Praise for
Winning Together

"Many have tried to write books about winning that parallel the sporting experience and lessons learned. However, Kate and Helen's book manages to translate some of the more intangible precursors for success and describe them in a way that would be useful to another athlete or someone starting their first job in the business world. This book is human, warm and a welcome addition to the bookshelf of any person looking to learn from their remarkable example."

John Amaechi, Psychologist

"This is the inside scoop, the real-deal on how to build winning cultures that keep people at the heart of things. The articulate details and storytelling from athletes and leaders who have walked the path is a must-read for anyone interested in contemporary performance leadership."

Dr. Pippa Grange, Psychologist & Culture-Coach

"Finally! A book that takes a different perspective on success and leadership. Kate and Helen's incredible story shows how there is a new emerging model of how to build a successful and authentic team environment – whether at work, on the sports pitch or at home. How honesty, vulnerability, conflict and ambition can co-exist to produce extraordinary results for the team and the individuals. And even maybe change the world a little bit for the better."

Michele (Mitch) Oliver
Global VP Brand & Purpose – Mars Incorporated
Vice Chair Stonewall

"Kate and Helen's story is hugely inspirational, told with such refreshing honesty and humility - a must read for anyone seeking to build a world class team and ultimately achieve outstanding results."

Clare Gilmartin
Former CEO Trainline and VP eBay Europe

"This book is both relevant and important for people who want to be part of high performing diverse teams. Helen and Kate see the opportunity for a more holistic way of working and functioning as people and teams. The future is going to require an enhanced style of leadership and this book will certainly help everyone on this journey of growth."

Maggie Alphonsi, Rugby World Cup Winner

"Powerful … Essential reading for anyone that's part of a team."

Matthew Syed, Bestselling Author

Winning Together

Winning Together

*An Olympic-Winning Approach to
Building Better Teams*

HELEN RICHARDSON-WALSH
AND
KATE RICHARDSON-WALSH

First published in Great Britain by John Murray Learning in 2021
An imprint of John Murray Press
A division of Hodder & Stoughton Ltd,
An Hachette UK company

1

The acknowledgments on pp. 199 constitute an extension of this copyright page.

A CIP catalogue record for this title is available from the British Library

Hardback ISBN 9781529316148
eBook ISBN 9781529316162
Audio download ISBN 9781529316131

Typeset by KnowledgeWorks Global Ltd.

Printed and bound in Great Britain by Clays Ltd, Elcograf S.p.A.

John Murray Press policy is to use papers that are natural, renewable and recyclable
products and made from wood grown in sustainable forests. The logging and manufacturing
processes are expected to conform to the environmental regulations of the country of
origin.

John Murray Press
Carmelite House
50 Victoria Embankment
London EC4Y 0DZ

www.johnmurraypress.co.uk

For Pfeiffer,
The sparkle in your eyes and the fire in your soul.

Contents

About the authors

Helen Richardson-Walsh is a double Olympic medal-winning British hockey player, winning bronze at her home Games in London 2012 and gold at her final Olympics in Rio 2016 – where she was one of only two players to score during a tense penalty shootout in the final. Having played international team sport for eighteen years, including in four Olympic Games, her knowledge of high performing teams and what it takes to win as individuals and teams is world leading. Her experience and insight into team culture and helping people thrive is supported with an MSc in Organisational Psychology which uniquely blends the sporting and academic worlds in her work with sports organisations and businesses. She powerfully shares her experiences of mental health and being LGBTQ+ as a passionate activist and supporter of equality and justice for all people. Helen is a proud Mum to Pfeiffer alongside her wife, Kate.

Kate Richardson-Walsh is a double Olympic medal-winning British hockey player who captained her country for thirteen years and represented Great Britain in four Olympic Games. Winning bronze at London 2012, having suffered a fractured jaw early in the Games, Kate finally stood at the top of the podium with her teammates in Rio 2016. Experiencing the rollercoaster of international team sport for eighteen years provided her with exceptional knowledge of team culture, leadership and people. Kate now uses her insight and expertise to help teams and individuals thrive in both sport and business settings. As one half of the first same-sex married couple to win Olympic gold together, Kate is a proud LGBTQ+ activist and a supporter of human rights causes. Kate is a proud Mum to Pfeiffer alongside her wife, Helen.

Foreword

There is so much more to sport than what happens on the field of play and a treasure trove of golden lessons to be learned from winning and, even more importantly, from losing.

Central to it all and something very few people can understand and even fewer can describe is how you build a strong foundation that can withstand failure and that is on course to the sort of success that can be enjoyed by everyone because every team member feels valued and has contributed to the cause. How you support teammates, how you pick yourself up from disappointment, how you use mistakes to fuel your energy to put things right in the future, how you enjoy the process of working towards a goal just as much as lifting the trophy at the end of it all. This book is a guide for life written by two people that I respect and revere.

Kate and Helen Richardson-Walsh have been there in the heart of the action and the heat of the spotlight as crucial parts of the team that won Olympic gold in Rio, beating The Netherlands in a thrilling penalty shoot-out that had 10 million people watching hockey, many for the first times in their lives. It was my favourite moment of the Rio Games and when I interviewed the team for the BBC on the following day, I wanted to hug each and every one of them. More than that, I wanted to be in their team. I was desperate to be one of them and I know I represented many women and teenage girls, hopefully men and teenage boys as well. I have never played hockey in my life but that's not the point – I wanted to be in their gang.

That's what Kate and Helen helped create: that magical, glorious feeling of shared elation and a renewed vigour to be the best in whatever way you could, both for yourself and for those around you. There was always a bigger vision to what that GB hockey team was trying to create. The gold medal was the target, but the prize was bigger than that. This was the first British team I remember being bold enough to state an intention and to commit to a cause. Their declared mantra was: 'Be the Difference, Create History, Inspire the Future'.

Even if the odds were stacked against them in the final and the Dutch had already booked the party venue to celebrate winning gold, that shared set of values made Team GB bigger and better than the sum of their parts. That victory had been built on the practice pitches of Bisham Abbey, in the gym and in the shared discussions about what they wanted and how they could achieve it. They had visualised everything, practiced every element, including taking penalties to the point where it became routine so that when it happened for real, they felt they had been there before. Whether it was those stepping forward to take the penalties or Maddie Hinch protecting her goal like an armoured giant on springs, every individual performed with confidence and calmness.

There is an art to absorbing pressure, enjoying expectation and keeping your cool in the moments when others might panic. It is a skill that can be learned and this book will help you do exactly that.

When Kate carried the flag at the Closing Ceremony for the Rio Olympics, she did it on behalf of every single member of her team and every one of us who had been inspired by their performance but my connection with Kate and Helen goes back further than that.

During the glorious summer of 2012, when we all bathed in the golden glow of the London Olympics and Paralympics, I made the most of any time off to go to different events. I sat in the stands at the hockey to watch the GB women play their penultimate group game against China. Kate Walsh (as she was then), had been smashed in the face with a stick in their opening game. Helen Richardson (as she was then) took over as captain for two matches. She kept the show on the road as Kate was taken to hospital with a broken jaw and had surgery. No one watching from the side-lines expected her to take any further part in the Games. Only Kate and her teammates thought differently. She came on with a face mask and I have to admit, I gasped at the courageous way she played in that game and in her determination to lead that team all the way to the bronze medal.

Courage is a word that often comes to mind when I think of Kate and Helen, the first same-sex married couple to win an Olympic gold medal for Great Britain. In a world where many still feel the need to hide their sexuality, Kate and Helen have led the way as LGBT role models. They do so in the full knowledge of the issues at stake. They recognise vulnerability and shame, they can empathise with those who find it difficult celebrate their own identity and they can show clarity to those who might struggle to discuss personal issues. As mothers, they can also identify with those who are managing multiple tasks and a family life.

Helen has a Masters in Organisational Psychology and has always been fascinated by the power of the mind. She has a wisdom far beyond her years and an ability to understand why people behave in the way they do, always with an innate kindness and sense of care.

Together, Kate and Helen are the ultimate team – supporting each other with honesty, thoughtfulness, consideration and clarity. Now they are sharing the lessons they have learned for the benefit of all of us. I am so glad they have written this book and I am proud to know them.

Clare Balding

Timeline

All events relate to both Kate and Helen unless otherwise specified. Asterisks signify tournaments played in.

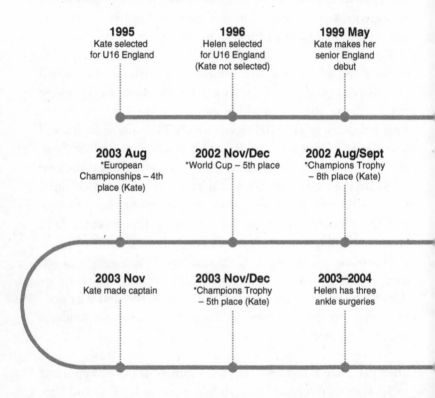

1995
Kate selected
for U16 England

1996
Helen selected
for U16 England
(Kate not selected)

1999 May
Kate makes her
senior England
debut

2003 Aug
*European
Championships – 4th
place (Kate)

2002 Nov/Dec
*World Cup – 5th place

2002 Aug/Sept
*Champions Trophy
– 8th place (Kate)

2003 Nov
Kate made captain

2003 Nov/Dec
*Champions Trophy
– 5th place (Kate)

2003–2004
Helen has three
ankle surgeries

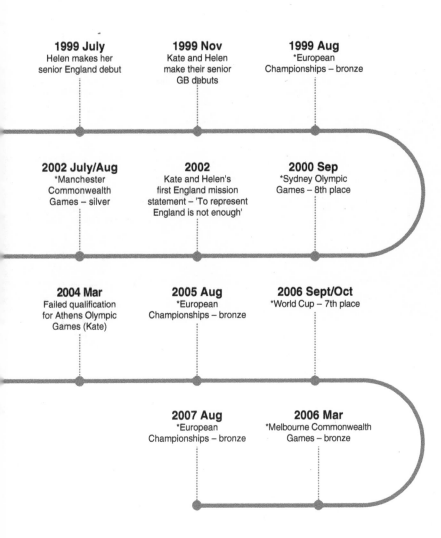

1999 July
Helen makes her
senior England debut

1999 Nov
Kate and Helen
make their senior
GB debuts

1999 Aug
*European
Championships – bronze

2002 July/Aug
*Manchester
Commonwealth
Games – silver

2002
Kate and Helen's
first England mission
statement – 'To represent
England is not enough'

2000 Sep
*Sydney Olympic
Games – 8th place

2004 Mar
Failed qualification
for Athens Olympic
Games (Kate)

2005 Aug
*European
Championships – bronze

2006 Sept/Oct
*World Cup – 7th place

2007 Aug
*European
Championships – bronze

2006 Mar
*Melbourne Commonwealth
Games – bronze

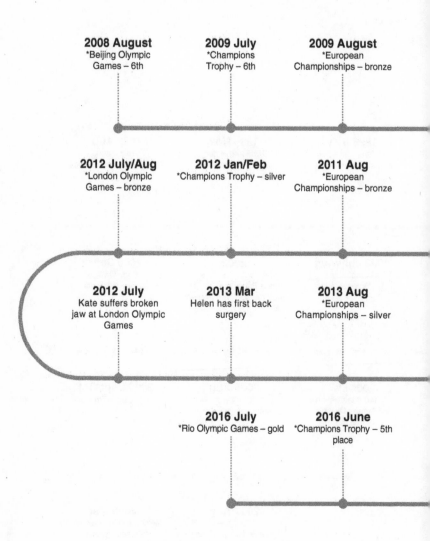

2008 August
*Beijing Olympic
Games – 6th

2009 July
*Champions
Trophy – 6th

2009 August
*European
Championships – bronze

2012 July/Aug
*London Olympic
Games – bronze

2012 Jan/Feb
*Champions Trophy – silver

2011 Aug
*European
Championships – bronze

2012 July
Kate suffers broken
jaw at London Olympic
Games

2013 Mar
Helen has first back
surgery

2013 Aug
*European
Championships – silver

2016 July
*Rio Olympic Games – gold

2016 June
*Champions Trophy – 5th
place

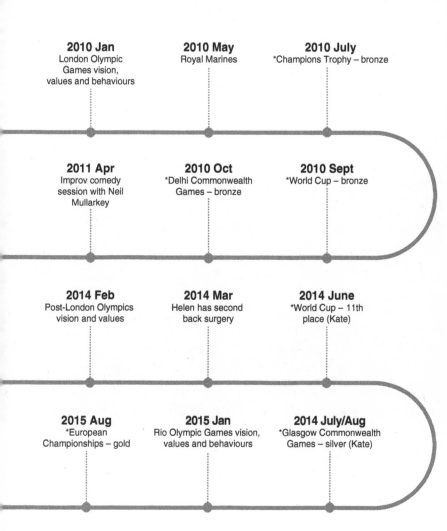

2010 Jan
London Olympic
Games vision,
values and behaviours

2010 May
Royal Marines

2010 July
*Champions Trophy – bronze

2011 Apr
Improv comedy
session with Neil
Mullarkey

2010 Oct
*Delhi Commonwealth
Games – bronze

2010 Sept
*World Cup – bronze

2014 Feb
Post-London Olympics
vision and values

2014 Mar
Helen has second
back surgery

2014 June
*World Cup – 11th
place (Kate)

2015 Aug
*European
Championships – gold

2015 Jan
Rio Olympic Games vision,
values and behaviours

2014 July/Aug
*Glasgow Commonwealth
Games – silver (Kate)

Preface

On 19 August 2016 we stood alongside our teammates on top of the podium as Olympic champions. What did our victory mean? What did it take to get there? And what did we learn along the way? Our experiences have led us to be fascinated by people and teams, why some succeed and others do not, and to question success itself. By sharing our story with you we want to help you reflect on your own experiences, gain some lightbulb moments of your own and grow in your personal and team performance.

For us, the 2016 Rio Olympic gold medal was 18 years in the making. We both represented our country from 1999 to 2016. Over a period spanning almost half of our lives we willingly gave all of ourselves in pursuit of greatness and the ultimate prize. To finally stand on top of that Olympic podium with our teammates, after all that we had been through, was monumental. Throughout our international careers we experienced an inordinate amount: winning and losing as individuals and as part of a team; captaining and leading teams; the importance of mental health and psychology; how to get the best out of yourself and others; embracing difference; thriving in uncertain times and finding calm in chaos.

A lifetime of hard choices and our Olympic dream came down to one moment – a penalty shootout against the Dutch. This was a chance to make history and become the first GB women's hockey team to win Olympic gold …

KATE: I stood at the end of the row on the halfway line. Hannah Macleod on my right-hand side, arms around one another in a chain of support. We looked on as our penalty takers stood with our coach, Karen Brown, and in the distance our goalkeeper, Maddie Hinch.

Each team had taken four penalties, and we were one nil up. It was on a knife edge. The tension was palpable in the stadium. We gripped each other a little tighter. I don't think I've ever felt as calm or still. One of our defenders, Hollie Webb, stepped up, the label of her shirt flapping in the gentle breeze of the Rio night, and waited for the umpire to blow her whistle and signal the start of her eight-second countdown. She drove into the circle, moved a little to her left, turned her back on the oncoming Dutch goalkeeper, spun to her right and then back to her left, the clock inching down. My neck craned to the right to try to get a better view. She released the ball on that spin, and the goalkeeper collapsed down onto the opposite side. The ball spun into the tightest of gaps between goalkeeper and goal post, millimetres between glory and disaster. The net bulged. A brief heartbeat of stillness. And then all at once a cacophony of noise and a maelstrom of motion, tired legs running, arms flailing, screaming, laughing, crying. We'd done it. We'd finally done it.

HELEN: Unbeknown to us, millions of Brits, now utterly invested, were watching all of this unfold back home. Families nervously gathered around their TV, hockey clubs were bubbling with excitement, and even football fans were tuning in down the pub. We've since heard many recollections of the cheers and celebrations that followed as we topped the Olympic podium and collected our medals. And then, as the people slowly went to bed and the cameras were turned off, we made our way back to the changing room one last time.

I sat up tall, my back flat against the newly tiled white wall, my thighs relaxed on the wooden bench while my feet struggled to reach the grey lino. Bags and sticks, towels, shoes and socks had been left strewn across the floor in the rush to take off our sweaty shirts and skorts to don Team GB's official podium outfit by Stella McCartney – all easier said than done! I could feel the dried-up sweat and grainy salt still clinging to my hairline, and I let out a deep sigh. I looked down. It was massive and shiny. It was so heavy. I could feel the weight pulling my head down and the ribbon digging into the back of my neck.

Finally. We'd done it.

I paused. I wanted to take it all in. To look at the incredible women beside me. To think about my heroes, the players not selected who had given everything to be sitting here but weren't. My family, the staff, coaches and teammates without whom I wouldn't be here. It was so quiet, except for the excited tapping of fingers on phones, as I was sitting completely content and serene. So this is it. This is what it feels like to be an Olympic champion. I caught the eye of my long-standing teammate and friend, Alex Danson, and shared a knowing smile before packing up my kit. Enough now.

KATE: It is easy to become fixated on 'that' game; after all, this is why we love sport. We are regularly asked questions about how we felt on the day of the Olympic final and what we did to prepare as a team in those last hours before the final. Rarely do people know or remember that we actually won all eight of our games out in Rio. Even more rare is the consideration of what got us there in the months and years prior to 'that' game. It does not have the glitz and glamour of an Olympic Games but the past is where the gold dust lies. Our hockey careers spanned five Olympic cycles and 38 international tournaments, including four Olympic Games.

The 'win' in Rio grabbed the attention and is hailed as the ultimate success. However, we know that we succeeded many times, in tournaments and in training, sometimes regardless of the score line. Winning is about more than medals and outcomes. We have titled this book *Winning Together* and have begun the book with us detailing our gold medal win in Rio, but for us winning is so much more than that. When we talk about 'winning' and 'success' in this book we mean these things in a much broader, holistic sense that includes, among other things, self-fulfilment and self-realisation. It is our experience of these longer-term 'wins' and our many failures that has enabled us to learn and grow as people and teams.

HELEN: It was because of those lessons learned that Kate and I both became a bit obsessed with teams, culture and people, and why we wanted to write this book. After ten years of inconsistent performances, I started to look over at the teams that were winning, wondering what they had that we didn't. I was convinced we had the hockey potential to beat these teams, but we rarely did. During this time, the subject of psychology was becoming more and more prevalent in every way. So I started to explore through continued experiential learning, but also formal education, the possibility of the impact our individual and collective minds were having on our results.

I have since learned that the power of the mind isn't all about unwavering belief and positive self-talk. It's about wavering but carrying on. It's about faltering and falling flat on your face but finding the courage to reflect and grow. It's about losing your confidence and still finding ways to perform. It's also about having the awareness to know your own mind and how it might be affecting your behaviour, and how that behaviour affects those around you. Our minds are our most powerful tool. When used effectively by individuals they can create great performances. But when mobilised collectively by a team of people, their power has the ability to make magic. It can create something so mind-bogglingly special you won't ever want to let it go.

Today, as an Olympic gold medallist, a psychology graduate and a master of organisational psychology, I can now see the difference between us and them, the thing that I wondered about all those years ago. It had nothing to do with effort or work rate; we did that as well, if not better than, anyone. It wasn't really to do with the stick and ball either. The most important aspect was what was going on in our minds, in every sense and every situation, including how we developed deep human connection based on truth and vulnerability.

KATE: Helen and I were completely invested in being better and doing better. This was particularly relevant for me over the 13 years I captained the team. Being made captain of the national team aged 23 was a baptism of fire to say the least, and it proved to be a steep learning curve. In many ways I never stopped climbing that curve. It got a little less steep over the years, but I was always thinking about where and when could I lead better. I made many thousands of mistakes, but the passion never really subsided.

My obsession with teams, leadership and culture was reflected in the books that I read, the speakers I listened to, and the people I interacted with. Helen and I have felt that we wanted to write a book about all that we have lived and learned for a long time. In fact, we have written this book many times, in our heads, on scraps of paper, during late-night conversations and on our computers. Each iteration of the book has had a slightly different feel. After much soul searching we decided that we absolutely needed to write what we wanted, in the way we wanted it to be written, and, most importantly, how we wanted it to be read. We hope that by sharing our lived experiences of teams it will help bring some of the key concepts of building a winning team to life for you.

It will quickly become apparent how totally obsessed we are with getting the best out of people and the teams they work in. In the years following that golden moment in Rio we have been invited into many teams and groups across diverse business sectors and sports. More often than not we are asked to share our thoughts on building high-performing teams, how we cultivated our culture, and what work we did on ourselves individually. There is so much in this book that is transferable to your teams because in the end it is simply all about *people*.

One thing we have come across frequently during our company visits is the lack of time people have and the need to focus solely on the day job, the deadlines, the targets and chasing the promotions. We get that – of course, we do. When you are constantly faced with Groundhog Day and a noses-to-the-grindstone mentality, giving time to your own growth and your team's culture can seem frivolous and unnecessary. However, we believe that those things *are* the day job. When you bring these elements of culture, awareness and leadership into your daily working life, and into your life more widely, it will help you be the person you want to be and the team you want to become.

HELEN: This isn't an autobiography, but we will use our own personal stories from an individual point of view and within the team context to draw out those key learnings. The actual moment of winning the Olympics, of course, felt amazing, but when I look back, that's not the moment I think about. I think about what we all had to do to make it happen, and the inspirational human connections I made along the way. That's what makes me most proud – being part of a team that had the courage to dare. Be vulnerable. We opened ourselves up and, in doing so, brought about the necessary change to take us from an average team that barely competed on the world stage, to eventually winning the highest accolade in hockey – Olympic gold.

One key component to our success was acknowledging the human element. We are all people. Every single person has a story that has got them to where they are today. We have all lived through unique experiences that have shaped who we are and how we see the world. Perspectives may differ, but we all yearn to be seen and valued. Recognising this lay at the core of how we tried to do things and how we tried to get the best out of ourselves and each other.

This has never been more relevant than in today's world, and it will only be those businesses and organisations that authentically invest in their people, be it employees or customers, that will live on. Decisions and choices are becoming more and more values based, and this book will challenge you to consider what this means to you.

This book really is for anyone wanting to improve themselves and their relationships. Of course, owing to the fact that our reflections and lessons mainly come from our time spent within a sporting context, it lends itself well to other sports teams looking to improve their performance, but it is just as applicable for understanding how any team, business or organisation, and even our own friendship groups and families, can flourish.

KATE: It is worth noting that this book is only two pieces of a giant puzzle. Although we all did the same training and sat in the same meetings, we all – players and staff – experienced them in different ways. These perspectives are all valid and important; they are people's truth and their lived reality. In this book we are candid and honest about our, Kate's and Helen's, points of view while protecting the sanctity of our team and our teammates.

This is our unique take as a same-sex married couple playing international hockey for the same team. We have faced splendid highs and desperate challenges. Not only have we faced these moments as teammates; we've lived them as friends, as individuals and as a couple. Many of our core beliefs and values are shared. But Helen and I are two beings, two brains, and this book reflects that and highlights our view that our difference is our greatest strength.

We wanted to share all that we have learned about building a high-performing team with you. Therefore, this book is for anyone who is a member of a team. We will play various roles in various teams throughout our lives, and we believe all of these lessons are applicable in every setting. We haven't always been explicit or joined the dots as to where our learnings might translate to your life because we want you to be free to do that work yourself. This book will hopefully make you curious about teams and prompt you to consider if, where and how you could be performing better.

To be anything less than the best version of yourself is to sacrifice the gift of life. We will argue that consistently successful teams are made up of people who are encouraged to flourish and whose individuality is welcomed. We want you to thrive, and we absolutely demand that you bring your whole brilliant self to all the teams you belong to. We will take you through our journey to better understand ourselves and, in doing so, hope that it might ignite a spark in you.

The book will be conversational: we will share our own personal experiences and reflect on our shared learnings. Each chapter is based around a key theme, and we will tell stories to bring these focal points to life. We have written the book this way with the intention of providing you with an in-depth insight into our world and what made us successful and at times unsuccessful. The value for you comes from comparing and contrasting our experiences with yours. By getting you to think in detail about your team's culture, yourself and your people in a new way we hope to be the check and challenge you need to get to the next level of performance.

Life is, after all, a team game, and, just as in a real-life team talk, you need some succinct bullet points to keep your focus. We are emotive human beings living in a fast-paced world, and a short task-focused synopsis can really make the difference to performance. So at the end of each chapter we will welcome you into our Team huddle and reflect back on the key learnings. The huddles are broken down into two sections: our hope is to prompt thought through the 'Questions to consider' and galvanise action through the 'Key team tactics'. We want these sections to make you think hard about yourself and the people around you. However you choose to read this book – working straight through, from beginning to end, or by diving into a chapter of particular interest to you – we hope it will provide you with moments of insight and contemplation and that individual chapters will serve as reference points for the future.

You will learn to win together.

Kate and Helen, April 2021

Introduction: This is what makes us

We've already said that this book isn't an autobiography, but nonetheless you'll find a lot about us as you read through its pages. Knowing and coming to terms with your story, your past, is important for understanding who you are and what you can be in the future. The vast majority of this book focuses on the period between 2009 and 2016, but here in this introduction we want to spend a bit of time introducing you to our younger selves, to our early lives as international sportswomen. After all, our experiences back then really shaped who we are as people today. We also want you to begin to connect with us as people – making connections is at the core of this book and at the core of being a team.

In this chapter we aim to provide a deeper insight into the people we were, where we came from, and what exactly it was about our lived experience that helped us achieve our goals. Over the years we have been forced to look back on our lives for various reasons such as tournament reviews, media interviews and motivational speaking engagements. This continuous rumination has provided us with a great deal of learning. At the same time, we want you to begin contemplating your own story, and what defining moments or pivot points are relevant to where you are now in your life. When we own our stories, and understand our 'why', it empowers us to write our own ending.

Finding purpose

KATE: It would be fair to say that, for the majority of our international hockey careers, Helen and I were obsessed with driving ourselves and the teams we played in towards excellence. We were dogged and determined. At times we were forthright and unyielding. Helen and I were both motivated by our past and our future in equal measure. We were hugely frustrated by our lack of consistency, and sometimes this was shown in a whole raft of emotions. Throughout it all, the team always came first, and we wanted everyone in that team to be the very best version of themselves because then, ultimately, we would all succeed.

HELEN: Our long, undulating careers have given us a unique perspective, and our varying experiences have taught us so much about hockey and life. Living for 18 years through four-year Olympic cycles provided us with natural points of reflection, and retirement from sport has given us some room to retrospectively assess it all. We started to wonder what and who made us think, feel and behave the way we did when we competed for England and Great Britain. By the end there was definitely a sense of urgency and desperation to win gold, but where had that come from? And what kept us motivated to keep going for 18 years? Although the values we hold deep to the core remain the same, the Helen and Kate who might have stood before you 20 years ago are very different from the ones who are here today. What were those big-impact moments that provided springboards for us to go to another level, to learn and grow as people and leaders?

KATE: My most impactful moment of growth came long before I'd even begun to dream about pulling on a GB shirt. It was my first real taste of disappointment in hockey that resulted in a colossal change of perspective on my life. I wasn't aware that this period of my life was to be so key to my hockey career and indeed my life at the time. At 15 years of age I had much more important things to consider!

Having started playing hockey in my PE lessons at Priestnall High School in Stockport aged 11, coached by the passionate Mrs Kinder, I progressed relatively quickly through the borough, county and territory system. Before I really knew what was going on, I was selected to play for England Under-16s aged 14. At this point in my life I had discovered boys and alcohol; it was what we did for fun at the weekend. I was eating a lot of junk food, and although I was playing hockey at Didsbury Greys HC, this consisted of only one training night a week and a game at the weekend. I didn't know what I wanted to do or be. I don't remember ever formulating hopes or dreams; this wasn't at the top of the priority list for the teachers at my state school, and so it remained low priority for me. I couldn't be a professional sportswoman because that didn't exist then, not really, and so the next best thing would be to teach PE and that is what I set about moving towards.

Playing for England Under-16s was great fun. I remember feeling out of my depth a lot but thought I added some value at times as well. After this first year I must have subconsciously thought that this would all happen again the following year. I clearly didn't think I needed to change anything I was doing because it had all worked out pretty well so far. Unfortunately, I got my wake-up call via the post and a letter that I've still got in the loft. I remember opening the selection letter in our hallway at home, seeing the All England Women's Hockey Association emblem at the top of the page and quickly casting my eyes down the page. What I found was a short blurb, which I barely took in, and a list of names in alphabetical order. My name was not one of them. That initial feeling of my stomach hitting the floor and then the heat of embarrassment and shame rising up my body are still palpable. I ran upstairs, locked myself in the bathroom, and sobbed.

They say you don't know what you've lost until it's gone, and this was most certainly the case here. When I eventually unlocked the bathroom door, my mum sat me down to talk about what had happened. I don't recall all that was said, but I'm almost certain I would have blamed the coach for dropping me and likely have favourably compared myself to other players who had made the team. My mum comforted me and then asked me a quite simple and yet brilliant question, 'What do you want to do about it, Kate?' I don't think I answered then, or indeed ever voiced an answer directly. However, with the support of both my parents and my coaches, for the first time in my life I started to seek out possible answers to that weighty question.

What transpired over the coming months and years was not a clear vision of where I wanted to get to or what end goal I wanted to achieve. It was more a mindset: the kind of person I wanted to be and how I went about my business as a hockey player and a young woman. I wanted to give it my all, be the very best hockey player I could and go wherever that took me. In the end, with the support of my family and a number of special coaches, it got me all the way to the very top. I learned so much about making hard choices, seeking out and listening to expert advice, the importance of challenging myself against the very best, loving the discipline of training and good nutrition, seeing how hard I could push my body and mind. Over the period of three years I went from missing out on England Under-16s selection to making my senior England debut and a year later representing Great Britain at the Sydney Olympic Games. As a result of that early disappointment, the transformation in me as a person and as a hockey player was phenomenal. I never forgot those lessons I learned as a young teenager, and somewhere deep down they drove me every day.

HELEN: It's so interesting to hear Kate reflect on that moment when she received the letter, because, while Kate was devastated, I was elated. Kate missed out that year, but I made the team for the first time. I didn't remember Kate from the trials, but when I turned up for my first England Under-16s training camp the chitchat from parents on the sidelines was about one thing: 'Kate Walsh hasn't been selected!' They were clearly surprised at Kate's omission, but I had absolutely no idea who this 'Kate Walsh' was! I shrugged and got on with the training, which is pretty much what I did from there on in: I just got on with it and I loved every moment. My rapid progression through the junior age group teams was seamless, and before I really even had time to think I was making my senior debut aged just 17 years old.

After one year of playing senior international hockey I also got selected for my first Olympic Games in Sydney 2000. Suddenly, in the build-up to these Games it all got very serious. The training started in September 1999, just as I was embarking on my final A level year. One week I'd be at college and the next I'd be at Lilleshall National Sports Centre with GB Hockey. This wasn't a huge sacrifice for me; I'd previously told my English teacher that, if it came down to a choice between training for an Olympics and completing my A levels, there would only be one winner; you can take your A levels anytime! Thankfully, with the help of our GB coach, Jon Royce, and some early planning I was able to do both ... just! But the stakes were high, and as the year went on, the anxiety of making selection silently grew and grew. Playing for my country – together with the overwhelming sense of human connection that comes from being part of a team – was slowly becoming something I couldn't live without – an addiction – and I didn't even know it.

Before the Olympics started, owing to a combination of my natural optimism, my inexperience and my knowledge that we had beaten all the top teams over the course of the year, I genuinely thought we could win it. When we struggled to play anywhere near to our potential and consequently failed to qualify for the Super Six stage of the tournament, I was absolutely devastated. It genuinely came as a bit of a shock. For the first time, as I wandered aimlessly around the Olympic Village one evening, I started to think about *what* I was doing and *why* I was doing it. What was the point to any of this?

This question was answered a few days later when I was watching the hockey final between Australia and Argentina. As I was sitting surrounded by my teammates and players from other losing nations, I tried to soak it all up and take in as much as I could. I wanted to fill myself with every last drop of knowledge, just in case. If this day was to ever arise, I wanted to be ready. The stadium was bursting. The crowd full of screaming Aussie fans all elated at seeing their team take on the home pressure and win the gold medal. I was still feeling gutted, lost and disappointed by our performance and overall finish of eighth, but when the Olympic anthem started to play and the medallists took to the field, goosebumps covered my body and I watched in awe. First the Netherlands, followed by Argentina and then the big one, Australia, were cheered onto the podium to receive their medals. Our manager, Chris Pickett, was sitting next to me. He turned to me and said, 'That'll be you one day.' With a steely look in my eye I stared down at the women standing on top of that podium, not the Argentineans or the Dutch, but those Aussies. I nodded to myself. Yep, I'd found the point, my reason, my purpose. I want to be an Olympic champion.

Until then, there hadn't really been an outcome focus to any of my thinking; it was very much about living in the moment. On witnessing first-hand the very best in the world, it made me reflect honestly on what I'd been doing up until that point and whether that would be good enough to achieve the goal of becoming an Olympic champion. It wasn't. At the time, I believed that some aspects were on point, but there was too much that wasn't. I know it's really easy to say you want to achieve something, but being prepared to actually do what it takes to get there is a different thing altogether. Only then, in that moment over two decades ago, did I begin to appreciate what it would take, and, most importantly, begin to take on the responsibility and willingness to do what I needed to get there. Knowing what I know now, from the luxury of being 20 years more experienced, barely anything I was doing at the time was good enough. However, the sentiment was exactly what I needed, and it was this that pushed me forward and to be the best I could be.

KATE: We all need a motivational nudge in the right direction now and again. Helen was training hard with good intentions, as we all were pre-2000. But we all needed to take a collective jump from good to great. We needed to stop being inactive bystanders in our own story and start being active creatives. As a young person in a new environment, it took some time to gain enough insight to form my opinions and help make progress happen. I, like Helen, was slowly coming to the realisation that something wasn't quite right and something big needed to happen. It was time to grab a pen and start writing the story in the way we wanted it to be written.

Hitting rock bottom

HELEN: The Sydney Olympics highlighted one of those things that weren't quite right – the Great Britain issue. Imagine training as England, Scotland and Wales for three out of the four years in an Olympic cycle, each nation with its own identity, vision, values, tactics and so on, and then with just one year to go before the pinnacle for your sport, the Olympic Games, you break up those teams to create a new one called Great Britain. That's how it had always been done, and it may sometimes have worked, but now, as sport headed towards a more professional era, it was no longer going to be good enough.

To Kate and me, as young people entering into a new world, the system seemed broken, and it created challenges that went way beyond having little time to generate a collective understanding of some tactics on a hockey pitch. Making a team takes way more than slapping a badge on some kit, and what we lacked was a real sense of *belonging*. We had three home nations coming together with their own agendas and heaps of baggage, and it was weighing us all down. Our inconsistency of performance was not because of a lack of intent or desire from any player or member of staff, but because our British identity was fragmented: with nothing to collectively identify with, together we had nothing to fight for.

I was beginning to understand what is important if teams are to succeed. Among others, Kate and I vocalised the need for a four-year GB programme, but when politics seemed to be getting in the way and nothing was changing, we were left feeling unheard and utterly powerless. What happened over the next four years made changes inevitable, but, unfortunately, we – the players and GB Hockey – collectively had to hit rock bottom to get there.

KATE: Rock bottom is one way to describe our fate in 2004. At times, it felt more like an abyss. We reached our collective nadir when yet another attempt to form a British team in a matter of months resulted in the GB women's hockey team failing to qualify for the Athens Olympic Games in 2004. It remains, to this day, one of my darkest and most haunting memories – we were making history for all of the wrong reasons. I learned a great deal from this failed qualification attempt, as a hockey player, a captain and a woman.

When the final whistle sounded at the end of our game against South Korea at the Olympic qualifying tournament in Auckland in March 2004, we knew that our Olympic dream was over. We could no longer finish in the top five at this tournament. We could no longer qualify for the next Olympics. The devastation feels as real to me now as it did then. I was utterly shellshocked, and my teammates and I were stunned; I had to physically help some of the players leave the field. It was like being trapped in a nightmare. This might sound like an exaggeration; after all, it's only sport. Except this was more than that: it was hopes dashed, dreams shattered, livelihoods lost, and the absolute end of international hockey for many of these women. None of us knew what the long-term effects of this devastating blow would be on GB Hockey, on England Hockey and on us as women.

This was one of the most testing periods of my hockey career, and as a captain it's the time I look back on as being a massive failure. I learned a lifetime's worth of lessons, but that couldn't bring those particular Olympics back. Growth didn't allow those players who retired after that Olympic qualifier to go back out and finish on the high they had wanted and deserved. I played and trained the rest of my career with these feelings fuelling me. I couldn't right those wrongs for those incredible women, but I wanted to make sure that it never, ever happened again. So part of my purpose of being the best hockey player and captain I could came from a desire to represent those women, to redeem their legacy and, personally, never go back there again. This was reflected in the way I communicated, the level of detail in my thoughts, the desperation in my actions and total obsession with always needing everything to be better.

HELEN: I followed the 2004 Olympic qualifier and that final game back home via vidiprinter-type updates on the tournament website. I felt numb just thinking about what my friends and teammates must be going through on the other side of the world. As this horrendous ordeal unfolded for them, I wasn't there with them because, for the previous 18 months, I had been fighting a personal battle.

In the summer of 2003 I was told I would never play hockey for Great Britain again. By that point, having already had one surgery on my left ankle, I was on the brink of returning to play when something went ping. For a split second the pain was excruciating and then I realised I could no longer move my foot out to the side. My peroneal tendon, the one that runs down the side of your leg and under your foot, had snapped in half. I got a second opinion about my prognosis, but the consultant still said that, while he could fix it, my ankle would never be strong enough to withstand the training required for international hockey. Needless to say, I didn't let *him* operate on me!

I needed a total of three operations, with the last one extracting a bit of my hamstring to weave in and out of my tendon to make it as strong as possible. In the end I couldn't play hockey for two years, and this was a challenge that tested every fibre of my being. The hardest part was being excluded from the one thing that I loved doing. It felt like this thing that I'd unknowingly become dependent on had been ripped away, and, to begin with at least, there was nothing I could do about it. I found it extraordinarily painful to watch my club team, Leicester: being part of that team but not really. I was jealous that I couldn't do what my fellow team members were doing and always felt slightly on the outside, however nice anyone was to me. As Kate has already said, it might sound a bit melodramatic – it's only hockey after all – but it was my life. It was everything to me, the only thing I knew. It *was* me.

An endless array of emotions fluctuated in and out at various points. I'd get upset at the most stupid things, and the uncertainty was overwhelming, but then I would be filled with gratitude for what I did have and love. I would flit from feeling dejected and sometimes resentful to feeling focused and determined. There were times I felt lost, and then I'd immediately get an attack of shame for feeling that way. I was galvanised and motivated by the deep desire to overcome these gargantuan obstacles. Anger, too, kept rearing up, and I hated it. I had felt let down by the medical profession and some of the advice I was given. I was convinced that a poorly advised and executed cortisone steroid injection had caused my tendon to rupture, and this kept popping into my mind. Eventually, in time, I managed to find some sense of peace and was able to move on.

This enforced time away from sport allowed me in some way to grow mentally, emotionally and physically. As with any serious injury, there are no shortcuts to full fitness, and spending hours upon hours doing mundane, slow, boring rehab exercises educated me about my body, and the gradual increase to full training taught me how to push myself farther than I ever had before. In a nutshell I learned how to train properly, and I returned stronger, fitter and leaner. Before the injury I saw myself as a hockey player; now I felt like an athlete. With a heightened level of gratitude for the sport that I loved, mentally and emotionally I was now more determined and single-minded than ever.

Hope springs eternal

KATE: We were both determined to turn this catastrophic situation into motivation for a better future. I found it very hard, emotionally, watching the Athens Olympic Games and not taking part. There was also an element of needing to be patient and allowing events to unfold, and this I found even harder. As a result of the women's non-qualification and the men not faring too well in Athens, as a sport, we lost 70 per cent of our UK Sport government funding. We were disparate and in need of some dramatic changes.

Then, quite serendipitously, just as we were assigned a new coach, Danny Kerry, London was awarded the Olympic Games for 2012. Danny was a young, relatively inexperienced coach at this level and inherited a disconnected group. I think he very quickly realised that he had an awful lot of work to do to help turn this ship around and steer us towards brighter horizons. He had a vision to improve our world ranking by one place each year, which ticked the funding body boxes and gave us, as players, something to work towards.

For Helen and I, though, the pace of progress seemed a little too gradual. We – the players – were still working or studying while training when we could at weekends or by taking time off. I personally felt like I wasn't able to give all of myself either to my career or to hockey; it was an impossible balancing act. It was hugely frustrating, and I felt like we were constantly taking one step forwards and two steps backwards. We finished sixth at the Beijing Olympics in 2008, which was enough to ensure funding for the next Olympic cycle but not enough in any other sense. Yes, it was closer to those elusive medals, but in reality we were still so very far away. We needed to do things differently and perhaps embark on something that had never been done before.

A fresh beginning

HELEN: The London Olympics was the perfect catalyst for this change, and if ever there was a time to take control and own our story this was it. A home Olympic Games was a once-in-a-life-time opportunity, and an opportunity too good to waste. The timing was perfect, and we were hungry to make the most of it. In 2008, when Danny floated the idea of a full-time GB centralised programme, referencing the continued success of the GB Rowing and Cycling teams that we needed to emulate, my instinct was to say 'Where do I sign?' I had been working lousy part-time jobs to allow me to train as full-time as I could, and stuffing envelopes in a tiny broom cupboard for British Judo for £6 an hour didn't quite have the same appeal. The prospect of going full-time didn't create that buzz for everyone. For a hockey squad to train full-time for nigh-on four years, as Great Britain, was a seismic shift, and we were each being promised a maximum of £12,000 per year in Lottery funding. Financially it was going to be a tough choice – for those who had been giving it their all for some time, trying to balance careers and families alongside playing hockey, the decision to move to a centralised programme would, more than likely, spell the end of their international careers. We inevitably lost players, and the consequence was that we started the London Olympic cycle in 2009 with a relatively inexperienced training squad. What we did have in abundance, however, was a group of strong, ambitious women who weren't content with the status quo, and even though we weren't entirely sure what it would take just yet to change that status quo, we were prepared to do it.

For Kate and I, after all the years of ups and downs, the injuries and surgeries, the losses and Athens non-qualification, the inconsistent performances and the not knowing what team would 'turn up', moving to a centralised programme was an absolute no-brainer, but it caused a bit of a stir within the hockey world. Some simply didn't agree with the whole idea, and we were quite heavily criticised by players and coaches from around the world and, sadly, from closer to home, too. Comments such as 'You'll be burnt out by the time the Olympics comes along' or 'You'll get fed up with one other' were made time and time again. It was a 'mistake', and it wouldn't work. But the way we saw it was as if, as a sport, we'd been thrown a lifeline. London being awarded the Games didn't just secure funding, it produced the biggest investment we, as hockey players, had ever seen. Surely the *only* way forward for this group was to train full-time at a central base, at the very least to justify the investment we were going to get from UK Sport.

KATE: I experienced this nay-saying first-hand, when I was mocked by two male hockey players in a hotel lift at a tournament in 2009 just as we were forming our centralised programme. This could have been quite intimidating, but I remember feeling absolutely certain that we were taking the right course of action for us. The entire squad needed upskilling in lots of areas on and off the pitch to compete consistently with the best, and our full-time programme was going to provide us with the means to do that. When the lift arrived at my floor, I simply turned and said, 'We'll see.'

HELEN: The external doubters proved to be a helpful galvanising force and over time helped us form a tighter unit. There was, at last, a sense of urgency among the group of players and staff to really grip this opportunity and serge forwards together. We had the beginnings of a unified team that was grounded firmly in our collective identity. Just being physically together on a daily basis would not be enough to take us all the way to the very top. What followed was the building of our culture and the making of us.

KATE: It certainly was a new beginning and a fresh start led by our management team and players. It was like a mini revolution, and it felt good. It was bold of our coaches to devolve some of the leadership and power to the playing group, and it was certainly a modern management strategy. In comparison to years gone by, in fact, this collaborative style of leadership could not have been farther removed from what we had experienced for much of our career to this point. The leaders we follow shape us: they shape the way we think and the way we behave. Whether leaders want this power or not, it exists and we must all be mindful of who we are affecting and how we are impacting on their lives.

Learning from our past

HELEN: As a hockey player, the leaders I most came into contact with were my coaches. The vast majority of coaching and feedback I received from an early age right through to the England junior squads and GB seniors was very direct and, at times, aggressive. My first memory was aged eight when I was told I couldn't wear gloves when the temperatures were freezing because I wouldn't be able to feel the stick. There were those that could 'handle it' and those that were 'weak'. As I got older, a consistent cause for anxiety were video meetings, or 'video nasties', as they became known. We all became adept at scanning each new clip, praying we weren't anywhere to be seen, then allowing ourselves five minutes of calm until the next clip. We weren't eager to learn and grow; we were hoping to survive then escape. Witnessing a teammate forced to wear a metal bin over her head because she got an answer wrong made sure of that. Looking back, we can see that these environments were built on fear and shame. They were abusive and dehumanising. They said, we did – or at least tried to – and if you didn't or couldn't, you got shouted at and humiliated. It was that simple, and as the fear grew my personal agency struggled to bloom.

KATE: My experience of coaching resembled Helen's from England Under-16s onwards, and I endured similar direct and aggressive coaching styles. At a Three Nations tournament in the Netherlands aged 15, the coach stood up mid-game, held up a stick like a rifle, and shouted that he would shoot me if I made that error again. I was made to kiss a teammate's feet mid-training session by one coach, because I kept passing her the ball. I was 17. I have been singled out for the 'hairdryer treatment' and heard every profanity in the English language used towards myself or a teammate. This kind of abuse marked much of my experience as a young player and undoubtedly left a trace on me. Not every coach was like this, of course, and indeed some coaches changed their style over time. But this was coaching in the 1990s and early 2000s, and this was the experience for a lot of athletes across sports. As a young woman, I felt like I had no choice but to take it all and carry on if I wanted to achieve my goals.

HELEN: I couldn't agree with Kate more. As young players, and not so young players, because we so wanted to get selected for teams and tournaments, it really felt as though we had no other choice – as athletes we are inherently vulnerable. Even though at times I would thrive on the pitch in that culture, as I look back now, it's difficult to understand why we put up with some of the more extreme training methods. I remember coming home from an Under-21s training camp when I was 15 years old and locking myself in the bathroom because I just needed to let it all out, which was very out of character for me. As the tears rolled down my face, I questioned whether I wanted to do this anymore. Hockey was everything to me, and yet here I was wondering if I could deal with it. And that was sport. The power imbalance was, and still can be, scarily one-sided. As a result, I always struggled to communicate with my coaches. Trust was something that never came naturally to me, and these experiences made this even harder. The barriers came up, my defence mechanisms working in full flow, and I just couldn't let them in.

Even though it was that way for me, as is often the case, what is done to you, you do to others, and to a large extent I took this way of doing things forward into how I would communicate with others, especially on the pitch. If a teammate didn't do something well enough, in no uncertain terms they'd know about it. As I got older, thankfully I listened, I learned and I grew. I realised that this way doesn't work for everyone; in fact, it works for very few people at all, and there is a better way.

KATE: We both agree that how we were coached occasionally prompted how we behaved as players. We're not proud of the way we behaved or communicated at times. There were certainly times when we overstepped the mark with things we said, particularly in training in the heat of the moment. We both believe that we always wanted the best for the team and our teammates. We are thankful and grateful that, on the whole, teammates understood our intent. Our experiences of volatile coaches are in no way an excuse for how we behaved on occasion, but they have helped us understand why we are the way we are. Over time we learned and grew ... though some might say not enough. In the end, those relationships we built with our teammates were very important to us both. And, as leaders, we definitely tried to understand the impact of our words and actions. As Maya Angelou puts it so beautifully, 'When you know better, do better.'

All this serves as a veracious account of how the past affected our present and how we chose to translate this into transformative purpose for our future. As we move through life, enjoying the highs and enduring the lows, we have the power to make the best of it all. We are the masters of our story because it's not what happens to us but how we interpret what has happened. We are all storytellers and we all have an incredible story to tell, and by framing that narrative in a positive way it can help us all live more purposeful lives. Furthermore, when our lives have meaning, when we have real purpose, we are much more likely to tell our story through the lens of growth, belonging and positive influence.

Now you have a better understanding of us, and hopefully yourself, we will move on to team culture. Specifically, the first three chapters proper of this book will look at what cultural factors led to our most consistent period of success. We will show how a collective vision, underpinned by meaningful values and brought to life by agreed behaviours, took us to the very top. The first and most important step is finding your vision, and that is where we will head to in Chapter 1.

Team huddle

Your past experiences have shaped the person that you are today. How you view your past experiences both consciously and subconsciously shape how you approach life and your relationships with other people. Reflecting on your story will help you get a better understanding of yourself. Giving time to understand other people's stories will provide you with important insights into why they are the way they are. Sharing your story with others is also a vital way we build trust with others.

Questions to consider

- Ask yourself the question 'What do you want/need?' And then ask yourself, 'What are you going to do about it?' Write any thoughts down and date the page.
- How long have you worked in the same organisation or industry, and what impact, if any, has this had on your thoughts, feelings and actions?
- How has your biggest success to date shaped you as a person?
- How have some of the challenging periods in your life shaped you as a person?
- Do you think any of your experiences affect how well you connect with your teammates?

Key team tactics

- Before any exercise where individuals are encouraged to disclose personal accounts, be mindful that sharing this level of vulnerability does not sit comfortably with everyone, so be thankful for all levels of participation.
- Telling your story is a powerful thing, but first you need to build it, then own it. Consider how certain experiences in your life have helped form who you are today,

then as a team share your own story in whatever way you like. You can use different mediums to help – life writing, drawing, drama, even Lego!

- If you feel able, share one or two pivot points or springboard moments with your team and encourage them to do the same. Getting to know someone personally will help build trust and respect and strengthen relationships. Although how we behave should not be easily excused by our experiences, it will provide some background and help build empathy for ourselves and others.

- Identify similarities and differences in your team and celebrate them both.

I
Team vision

Creating a collective vision and sense of belonging can mean the difference between standing on the Olympic podium and not even qualifying. There are many pieces required to create success, and a team vision is just one part of that jigsaw puzzle. However, the vision is fundamental: it is the corner pieces of the puzzle and needs to be laid down first. How can you begin any journey if you don't know where you're heading? A vision is what gives you that ultimate destination, whether that be tangible or metaphorical. Most importantly, it provides clarity of direction, and, if done well, can create meaning, enhance motivation and provide a sense of belonging.

Of course, team visions and group mission statements are not new or ground-breaking concepts. There are many hundreds of research papers and books dedicated to this very topic. What we want to explore in this chapter is how our various experiences of a central team purpose shaped our successes and to some extent our failures. It is not only the vision in and of itself that is key; it is how the vision is formed and the ultimate power of shared understanding.

We didn't always know how important the vision was to our team success. In fact, we first had to have it and then lose it to fully appreciate the significance. This eventually led us to the memorable and meaningful team vision for the Rio Olympic Games: Be the Difference, Create History, Inspire the Future.

But how did we get to that point and how can what we learned help you build the best vision for your team? We think this is applicable to any and all team environments you find yourself in, be that at your place of work, your netball team or your family unit.

Creating a sense of belonging

HELEN: In the years and decades before Rio we went through many different 'visions', 'goals' and 'mission statements'. If we ever had any of these for the Sydney Olympics in the year 2000, it's been lost in the mists of time. I remember we had a lot of detailed information around tactics for each game but nothing that went beyond the pitch. Sydney didn't go very well. We ended up finishing eighth out of ten, and the aftermath wasn't pleasant.

It was a few years before anything like a vision came along. When Tricia Heberle, former Hockeyroo and videographer during Australia's eight-year dominance under Ric Charlesworth, was appointed as the new England and GB coach in 2001, she brought fresh ideas. One of these was the importance of having a shared understanding of what we were about as a team. We all inputted into the process and what came out was the first team mission statement of Kate's and my playing career. This is what it looked like:

IF YOU THINK REPRESENTING YOUR
COUNTRY IS ENOUGH – DON'T BOTHER

IF YOU'RE PREPARED TO DIE FOR ENGLAND –
WELCOME TO OUR TEAM

TO REPRESENT ENGLAND IS NOT ENOUGH
We must play every game as if it is our first and every
minute as if it is our last

TO REPRESENT ENGLAND IS NOT ENOUGH
As one we stand alone but together we are strong

> TO REPRESENT ENGLAND IS NOT ENOUGH
> We must create an environment that embraces individu-
> ality and where everyone has a voice
>
> TO REPRESENT ENGLAND IS NOT ENOUGH
> Teamwork is about the ultimate sacrifice: there is no 'I'
> in team
>
> TO REPRESENT ENGLAND IS NOT ENOUGH
> Professionalism and lifestyle can go hand in hand; it
> depends if we are professional about our lifestyle
>
> TO REPRESENT ENGLAND IS NOT ENOUGH
> Each and every day we should strive to improve our-
> selves for the benefit of the team and bounce back
> stronger and better from any setbacks we may encounter

Looking at this now, with the benefit of distance and time, it's difficult to know what to think about it. Some of its do-or-die nature is a little cringeworthy; it feels a little jargon-heavy, but a lot of it really wouldn't have looked out of place in the versions that followed. It does reflect where we were at the time, though, and possibly where sport was as well. Mission statements galvanise a need for togetherness, teamwork, professionalism and a constant striving for improvement, something to get behind and fight for – a belonging. With no doubt, when these words provoked action, we achieved success through our improved performances on the pitch: a Commonwealth silver, beating the world's best team, Australia, in the semi-final; fifth place at the World Cup 2002, and qualification for our first ever Champions Trophy. We were improving, as was our greater sense of collective identity and sense of belonging.

However, if you're really on the ball, you might be able to spot one of the major problems with the mission statement. It's all about England. And of course it was – it was written by and for the England team competing between 2001 and 2003, so nothing wrong with that. This only became problematic the following year when the team aiming to go to an Olympic Games was, of course, Great Britain. We would have to go through it all again and hope that there was enough time to identify as one.

Groups of people won't always naturally mould into a cohesive unit; it takes time and effort to establish an identity, strengthen bonds and build that sense of belonging. But it's worth it, when we feel like we belong the chances are we'll perform much better.

Being on the same page

KATE: In that last year in the build-up to qualifying for the Athens Olympic Games in 2004 we must have gone through our team purpose again. My memory has faded somewhat but I can remember there being some conversation about a GB identity and really trying to bring the four Home Nations together. It was all very last minute, though, and as a result, looking back, it did not particularly have the depth we needed at this crucial stage of our preparation. As you know, from reading the previous chapter, we did not qualify for the Athens Games in 2004. There were, in my opinion, lots of reasons for this. In my experience it is rare for there to be one specific thing that goes awry that ultimately leads to a team failing. The collapse of Lehman Brothers and many other financial institutions in 2008 was not the result of one rogue person, one bad decision or one key moment. As with almost any team failure, there are a number of systemic errors, both large and small scale, that have catastrophic consequences. It is this, in the end, that brings the whole thing crashing down.

Certainly, one of those major elements is a collective vision. A central purpose that has been bought into and brought off the page by every member of the group. In 2004 this was one of the elements we lacked and was certainly in part responsible for the devastating events that unfolded out in Auckland at the qualifier.

It was a tournament like any other in terms of preparation and set-up. We were out in New Zealand in plenty of time to adapt to the time zone and surroundings. We prepared like we always did for every tournament I had been to so far in my career. On paper we should have been fine: five out of the 12 teams competing at the tournament would qualify for Athens. Despite our poor performance at the Euros with England in 2003, a fifth-place World Cup finish in 2002 along with some other good results had us ranked number one in the tournament (based on England as the nominated country). But we were here as Great Britain, a new team, so who knows where we ranked in reality?

All of our team meetings were conducted in our coach's hotel room as meeting rooms were expensive and hard to get hold of. So far so normal. And, just like normal, we sat all together a few days out from the tournament and had a meeting about what our goal was going to be for the tournament. There were some small group discussions and then feedback and discussion as a whole group. We were split, I think around fifty–fifty. Half of the group thought we should be going in with the purpose of winning the tournament. The thinking was: have high expectations and automatic qualification would be secured. The other half wanted to finish in the top five. Again, there would be automatic qualification but with some wiggle room and certainly lower expectations.

I honestly cannot remember how I voted or what I wanted. Looking back, it seems a no-brainer to me. Why not aim for the highest point you can? High expectations could mean greater endeavour, more diligence and better levels of performance. But, in context, looking at the team – at its confidence levels and individual and collective performance levels – finishing in the top five could seem like a more realistic and safer option. Goodness knows what the 'best' answer would have been; who knows if one answer was right and one was wrong? The only thing I do know now is that a disagreement on team purpose within the team can lead to only one thing – disruption and defeat. And, sure enough, it did. We left the room agreeing to disagree. When we walked out of that hotel room in Auckland, we sealed our own fate and we failed to qualify for the Athens Olympic Games in 2004.

I would love nothing more than to give you some other real-world examples here of how a lack of joint purpose resulted in failure or collapse, but in truth I would merely be postulating. Only those within the circle really know about causes and effects. I can speak only from my experience, and, of course, hindsight is a wonderful thing, and if I knew then what I know now perhaps it would have all played out differently. But I didn't know how vital that joined-up thinking was at this point in my life or career. We were all fighting fires in our own lives, all busy dealing with what was directly in front of us. I did not have that bigger-picture view. I knew that we desperately needed a four-year GB programme, and that was what we as players put a lot of our energies into after the failed qualification. In large part this was about time together on the hockey pitch, but it was also about that shared sense of identity and sense of belonging. We needed to be together, aligned and moving forwards as a collective. This is as true in business as it is in any sports team and is never more prevalent than when companies merge or a business is taken over. The alignment of a new purpose that encompasses all of the teams right at the start of any new merger will make or break the company's future.

A long and arduous review process followed, and the players tried to exert what little power we had on the GB Board by submitting a letter signed by the majority of the players.

We needed better processes, more astute and quicker coaching appointments, and, most importantly, a four-year GB programme. If we wanted to play as Great Britain and if we wanted to be taken seriously as an international team, we had better start taking it seriously. We couldn't be so arrogant or naive to believe that training sporadically for ten months in the lead-up to an Olympic Games was enough to do ourselves any justice. If there was one good thing to come out of not qualifying for Athens, it was that we as players had at least found a joint purpose and an understanding of where we wanted to go and how badly we wanted to go there.

HELEN: Unfortunately, those lessons weren't learned quickly enough, or maybe they got lost with a change in leadership at the very top of the Great Britain Hockey Association. During the Beijing Olympic cycle, we definitely played some matches as Great Britain throughout, which was a positive change. However, it wasn't until we were about six months out from the Olympics itself that we met to discuss our aims for the tournament. Even when we made time for a meeting, somehow, once again, we left that room without an agreement of what we wanted to achieve. Sounds familiar? Some wanted to try to win it; others wanted to be more 'realistic' and felt finishing in the top six would represent an improvement on our world ranking. Unsurprisingly, we ended up finishing sixth in Beijing.

Even as I write this, the dejection is washing over me once again. It's so bloody obvious now. For any team vision, goal or aim to be successful, you have to be on the same page.

Reaching for the moon

HELEN: This is why the London Olympics presented such an opportunity. With the decision to train full time, there was now time to give to, and work on, our culture. Finally, we could do something different and create exactly what we wanted.

To make this work, we needed everybody on-board and we needed everybody to be on the same page from the very start. We had two and a half years to grow and develop, but we needed to know where we were going and what we were aiming for. So, empowered by our coach, Danny Kerry, and led by our psychologist, Tom Cross, on a cold February morning in 2010, there I was sitting surrounded by a group of strong, ambitious women – my teammates – together with our staff, all of us tasked with the goal of agreeing on a team vision. Most significantly of all, this was a vision for Great Britain.

Rightly or wrongly, during the meeting I remember being quite forthright. The meeting we had in the lead-up to the Beijing Olympics was undeniably playing on my mind. When it comes to hockey, I've also been something of an optimist. Well, actually, I would say a realist, because whenever I stepped on to a hockey pitch, I always thought we could win. Never did I doubt the ability of any of the teams I played in. The possibility, the hope, the dream … I always believed it.

With that mindset, coupled with the pain and suffering, all the wasted talent and time that had gone before, all I kept thinking was that we absolutely could not leave this room without a) all of us being on the same page, and b) having a goal that was worth all the effort. It needed to be worth fighting for, something to inspire us, especially us oldies who had been there for a decade already. This time I wouldn't let this meeting pass me by without saying my piece.

Fair play to everyone, we all thrashed it out. Splitting off into small groups and then back into one big group multiple times, all the players and all the staff put forward their views and opinions. Have you ever been in open discussions like this with your team? It's worth a try if you haven't already done so – just make sure you keep your mind open.

What I was most grateful for was when people really opened up and shared their fears. I can still remember the atmosphere of the whole room; the fear of failure was palpable.

'But, but what if we don't win *gold*?'

In the previous Olympic cycle we were ranked between eighth and eleventh in the world, we hadn't won a world-level medal since 1992 – who were we to think that in two and a half years' time we could achieve the ultimate success in our sport? But now, for the first time in my career, we were talking about winning the Olympic Games.

The fear was understandable, and our lack of belief came across loud and clear in the reluctance to even utter *that* word. We said 'to medal', 'to podium', 'to be the best we can be' ... For hours we continued to discuss, challenge and argue our points of view, the positives and negatives, what our vision said to us, and to others, how it would make us feel and behave. But in the end we all committed to one word:

GOLD

The vision of 'GOLD' was born. But it was more than just a word. It was the sum of our discussions; it had meaning and purpose for each and every one of us. A team or company ethos can be encapsulated by a single word or phrase to good effect. Airbnb has a strong example: 'Belong Anywhere'. It's incredibly simple, and yet the brand's purpose is abundantly clear.

Tom was excellent at facilitating these discussions – it was essential for us to understand the perspective of everyone sitting in that room; those that would be living the vision and making it happen. We knew it wasn't going to be easy, but understanding where we were all coming from was fundamental to our success. It's also worth noting that it wasn't our coach, Danny, leading these discussions. As the person making selection decisions, he was acutely aware of his influence and he didn't want to sway the outcome, even accidentally – something for any leader to think about. Just being in the room as a leader can change how people behave and what people say. It's not always possible to change that fact, but being aware of it and actively seeking openness and honesty will help, and leading by example, of course.

KATE: Of course, it is more than likely that, having established our team vision at our training base, Bisham Abbey, that day, some players left with some doubts. It is realistic to assume that some players and even staff left that room not fully believing in our agreed central purpose. This is a reflection of where we were as a group and who we were as people in the group at that time. This was as much about the journey as it was the destination.

This time around we absolutely knew where we were headed whether we all believed it initially or not. By virtue of the fact that we had delved deeper into team values and behaviours that would support our vision of 'GOLD', it genuinely felt that we were finally aligned. When people are made to feel as though they are integral to the building and function of a team purpose, it creates a much greater sense of belonging. If team members feel that they can raise doubts and points of concern about the team vision, then that in itself is a good indicator of an excellent team culture. The questions and conversations promote clarity, and when it comes to team vision you cannot get any more crucial than that.

HELEN: Considering we are not double Olympic champions, you will know that we didn't win the gold medal in London. We finished third and took home the bronze, the first GB hockey team to do so since the 1992 Olympics in Barcelona. Having dedicated ourselves to 'GOLD' for all that time, this was utterly heart-breaking. On visiting many schools after the London Olympics, I was often asked how I felt about winning bronze. Once the initial disappointment and sadness subsided, I actually had an overall feeling of contentment. For the very first time in my career I could be satisfied in the knowledge that we had done everything in our power to the best we could be, the whole squad of 28 and all the staff. My definition of 'winning' was beginning to change. Don't get me wrong, I was still hungry for more, but in that moment that was enough for me. We reached for the moon, and that time we landed among the stars.

I know that wasn't true for everyone, though, and some struggled to deal with feelings of 'failure'. It's always a difficult balancing act, having a vision that is both aspirational and achievable, but it's important to remember that many of our minds make a habit of limiting our ambition, our ability, our greatness! I honestly believe that by stating 'GOLD' as audaciously as we did, we put it well and truly on the table. There were no ifs or buts; there was no doubt in anyone's mind.

So, don't be afraid to go for that lofty goal. Really, what do you have to lose? We all have our doubts, but when we're able to remove the limits that our brains often place on us, we're finally free to all the things we're truly capable of. Ask yourself this question: if you knew you couldn't fail, what would you aim for?

Forget the past and fail fast

KATE: As debriefs and reviews were part of our lives as athletes, we reviewed the London cycle. We filled in a survey and had the results read back to us by our external facilitator. At the same time we were feeding into a GB consultation aimed at allowing GB to compete as a team in all world-level competitions in the four-year Olympic cycle. We also had both the women's and men's head coaches apply for the Performance Director role. Plus, as athletes we found ourselves without funding for a few months as GB Hockey had pushed all the funding to pre-London to help us train full-time. So we were without a head coach, without funding. The women's squad had just won an Olympic medal and we were treading water, waiting. It was a hugely frustrating time for everyone involved.

The coaching merry-go-round spun round: our coach, Danny Kerry, was appointed as the Performance Director, and the men's coach, Jason Lee, was given the women's head coaching role. Danny and Jason are two very different people, with different approaches and different styles. Nothing wrong with being different, of course: it can bring a fresh new look and a sometimes much-needed new perspective.

As Helen has pointed out, the squad vision for London was really at the core of who we were and what we were about. We wanted to win, and we wanted to have fun doing it. It's fun when you win at whatever small or big level, as an individual and as a collective.

Visions are more than the sum of their words; they are the summation of a group feeling and must live off the page. When you read them, there needs to be a sense of attachment and belonging. Some may resonate with you in a positive way. Some you feel less attached to. If you asked every member of the group to describe how they feel about the joint purpose, odds are it will be slightly different – and that is their truth. The way we feel about a group goal is affected by our perspective, our role in the team and our outlook at that time. I, as an individual, might love our vision. You, as my teammate, may not think of it so fondly – the key is we all pledge to align ourselves to it.

The post-London training squad didn't establish a team vision until January 2014, nearly 18 months after the London squad had won that Olympic bronze medal. A lot of water had passed under the bridge in that time, and I was left feeling as if all the incredible hard work of players and staff in the build-up to London had been rather harshly dismissed. Again, that might not have been the intention but that was how I felt. I remember feeling completely lost, angry and really concerned about where we were heading. As a senior player and leader in the team I was acutely aware of my influence on other players and of my bias towards what had gone before. I very consciously and very pointedly tried to get behind the changes, the new 'way'. I always carried my doubt around, though, and those doubts grew considerably over the next year and a half.

When we finally did talk about our team vision, we did it just as before, with small groups bringing ideas back to the whole group for discussion. And so, on our tour to San Diego in January 2014, we cemented our vision as:

> Better than yesterday, striving for Gold

My recollection of this time was that we spent a lot of time on this trip thinking of 'fun' ways to document this vision. There was talk of a team song, players spelling out the words on a hockey pitch, a video of hands together over a poster of the vision. We spent a hell of a lot longer in these small groups coming up with these ideas than actually talking about how we were going to bring this vision to life in our everyday behaviours.

Of course, vision making should be a fun and collaborative exercise, but, more often than not, it's not the jazzy representation of that vision that carries weight or has meaningful impact, it is the conversations and discussions that help turn words into valuable actions. The connection between what those words meant and how they translated into day-to-day actions was lacking.

When as England we crashed out of the World Cup in the summer of 2014, placed 11th out of 12, it was no surprise – it had been coming. Did I give it my all? I absolutely did. Was I creating my own self-fulfilling prophecy around the outcomes of this group? I don't think I was. We were struggling and rudderless. *I* was struggling and rudderless. Our vision lived on a page in San Diego, frozen in time; it never lived or breathed in our group. Whose fault was that? Everyone's.

After this experience I fully believe that every group needs to respect what went before. Even if you decide on wholesale changes and a complete 180-degree change of direction, you at least owe it to those people in the room, and those who built what went before, whether it worked or not. Either way you learn, and either way you grow, together as the new team.

How do you want to be remembered?

HELEN: After the 2014 World Cup, Danny Kerry, first as an interim and then full-time, came back in as our coach, while continuing his role as Performance Director. However, before we could do anything productive, we needed time to heal. We needed it as individuals, and we needed it as a collective. As individuals this took many forms. Kate and I will discuss our own healing processes of widely differing experiences in 2014 in Chapter 9, on well-being, but as a group, in order to move forwards we had to address the pain and suffering that was eating at the heart of our team, and it had to be done together. Leading our conversation was an extremely experienced psychologist, and she had to be. Dr Kate Hays brilliantly facilitated the heated discussion. It was so important that all of the grievances we were all holding on to should come out in that meeting.

I will be forever grateful for that meeting. Many of us needed to ask for forgiveness. I know I did for the role I had played in what the team had become. It was possibly the most challenging meeting I've ever been in, and yet it was the making of us. I will never forget the way everyone showed up that day, either throwing metaphorical punches and/or taking them on the chin for the greater good. We were all being seen properly for the first time as this group of people. We were truly vulnerable. For that

I can't thank everyone enough. Being vulnerable within teams is something that doesn't come easily to many people, and certainly not within a competitive business world. But your ability to express your vulnerabilities is the key to unlocking your full potential as an individual, and as groups of people. This is something we discuss in more detail in Chapter 6.

Now we could set about forging a new vision for Rio, for which we still needed to qualify. In January 2015 we started this process. Although we were still bruised and a little battle weary, there was an altogether different feel. There was a sense of importance and urgency in the group. Along with Danny, Dr Andrea Furst, our new psychologist, set the scene and guided us into some incredibly vital conversations about our team culture. As it had been for the London vision, we were once again empowered to build it together.

As a group of 31 players and staff we were inspired by one simple question:

> How do you want to be remembered?

Everyone had a say. Over the course of about three months we talked, debated and discussed. We pitched our ideas and listened to other people's impassioned thoughts. This time we wanted our vision to go beyond tangible medals or rankings. We all felt that the last 18 months had taught us a lot about life and what was important to us as human beings. We wanted to pay respect to the past, the women and men that had gone before us and paved the way for us to be here in this moment. We wanted to look ahead optimistically to the future, where could we take this sport, what could we do for women's sport and what wider impact could we have on society. Most importantly of all, because we had just under 18 months to turn this ship around, our vision needed to be rooted in the here and now. We needed to be mindful and present. It was every single one of us in every single moment. Our vision for Rio:

> Be the difference.
> Create history.
> Inspire the future.

KATE: I love this vision wholeheartedly. I love it now as much as I loved it then in 2015. The reason I think this vision worked so well for us is because it's all encompassing and is about every member of the group. Success is multi-layered and multidimensional, and this vision accounts for that fact. We absolutely believed that the group could 'create history', and that in order to do so it would be about the whole group of 31 players and staff. In that sense, there was absolutely a pursuit of that elusive Olympic gold medal. At the same time there was room in this vision for success to be measured in other ways. The beauty of our vision lies in the ability for each and every squad member to feel empowered to define success on their terms. Not every member of the 31 players would physically make it onto the podium and yet that success is still theirs. As you'll read in the next chapter on team values, one of our values was explicitly about being a winner and how success could simultaneously be about winning a gold medal and any number of other meaningful outcomes.

Although I'm now long retired from the team and international hockey, this Rio squad vision is still my purpose. The vision is all of the things I believe a great vision should be. It is inspirational, it is unifying and it provides a clear focal point around which decisions can be based. It is neither perfect nor eternal and yet it is excellent. And that is exactly the type of vision you need to take you to where you want to go.

At the very least our team visions provided us with a sense of purpose and a clearer direction of travel for the group. Establishing what we wanted us to be about more broadly helped us form short-term goals with more certainty and form an understanding of what we were basing decisions on day to day. At their very best, our team visions gave our lives a greater sense of purpose and a genuine sense of belonging. When we were rooted in, and invested in our shared vision, we were stretched, developed and challenged. The shared knowledge of who we were as a team enabled us to have a greater feeling of worth as individuals.

Being empowered to build your own team vision isn't always possible, but getting under the skin of the existing vision and really connecting to it on a deeper level can impact you and your team in the most wonderfully powerful way. Establishing an ownership of your team vision will not only keep you motivated and focused when the storm clouds roll in, but will also importantly provide a spotlight to highlight the smaller successes. When you own the vision, you are responsible for driving the vision. That collective sense of purpose and of self-value that can come from an aligned group provides us with a basic human need we all desire: it gives us belonging.

This chapter will have aided you in taking the first major step towards great team culture. As we head into the next chapter, on team values, keep your own vision front of mind. It will serve as your most trusted guide, bringing your vision off the page and into real life.

Team huddle

Creating a vision should be the first step in shaping any team. Within any team, group, organisation or family, it is vital for everyone to be on the same page and heading in the same direction. The most effective way to create buy-in to the vision is to include all team members and empower them to own it. This is important in the building stage of a vision and in the day-to-day driving phase as well. The honest discussions and open conversations are of equal importance to the central purpose you've all bought into. Allowing team members to be honest about their doubts and fears about the vision is essential and will require a deep level of respect for one another's vulnerabilities. Like any good story, these candid conversations will enhance meaning and help to provide common ground long after any meeting has finished.

Questions to consider

- How do you want to be remembered as a team?
- Where is your team culturally, and where does it need to be?
- Is your team vision aspirational and motivational?
- Do you need a tangible vision or a 'bigger-picture' vision?
- How are you and your teammates bringing your vision to life, day to day?

Key team tactics

- Where possible, empower the whole team to build the team vision. At the very least, every team member should be able to own and drive the team vision. This will encourage responsibility and accountability of all team members and crucially foster a much needed sense of belonging.

- Giving time to well-facilitated discussion and conversation creates a deep level of understanding among the team. These exchanges embed a sense of trust that everyone is pulling in the same direction and therefore promotes togetherness.
- Be prepared to put yourself out there with a lofty goal. Don't be limited by current circumstances or what might be perceived as possible. An aspirational vision will inspire people to challenge themselves and their teammates with certainty and clarity. It will also help foster enthusiasm and commitment.
- Good, bad or indifferent, be respectful of what and who went before as there is always something to learn and it will help you create your future successes.
- Regularly review how, where and when your vision is brought to life. Celebrate the small milestones along the path to your team vision. Any and all success shows progression and progression is motivational.

2
Team values

Almost every organisation has its own company culture, and it is that culture that creates its identity and sense of what it is. The team vision, as you read in Chapter 1, plays a huge role in centring everybody in the team to the same point of how you want to be remembered. The team values, then, are the glue that bind a team together. Whether they are generic terms or unique phrases, once team members are on board with the team values, they provide clarity and have the ability to foster deep levels of trust.

That being said, hands up, who rolled their eyes when they saw the word 'values' at the top of this chapter? For many of us, team values have become so ubiquitous they have lost almost all meaning. In many cases we have become numb to the power of our team values. And yet we are increasingly basing many of our life decisions around values. It is imperative, then, that our values don't live only in company documents or plastered on giant posters or office screens. The power of collective authentic values is something we believe is a non-negotiable for any group or organisation today. From our experience, we were at our best when our team values lived and breathed in every member of the team. When our collective words became our collective actions, we brought values off the page and into real life. In this chapter we will discuss our experience of team values — what worked and what didn't work for us and why.

Time to talk

HELEN: If your vision is very aspirational, which hopefully it will be, it can sometimes feel out of reach by the time the excitement of making that vision has died down and you get back into the day-to-day routine. This is where your values come into play by bringing your vision into your daily lives.

Once our conversations got flowing in 2010 when we first started to consider our vision, values and behaviours for the London Olympic cycle, at some points it did get a little confusing to remember what exactly we were trying to come up with. It even felt a little overwhelming, especially for a real thinker like me.

According to the *Cambridge Dictionary* definition, values are 'the principles that help you to decide what is right and wrong, and how to act in various situations'. It can be helpful to have this definition close by when conversations get deep into the nitty-gritty, to help keep everyone's minds on track. It's a nice simple one: it clarifies what you're after, which is essentially to decide on what is 'right' and what is 'wrong', the best bit being that that is completely up to you. The most important thing to remember is that your values must link to your actions. They then help to provide direction and clarity around any decision-making processes and behavioural and ethical standards thereafter.

One thing I've learned, and something you need to know, is that coming up with strong values, and sticking to them, requires a backbone. They are not an easy fix – choosing a few words and calling them values will not suffice. They take time to get right in the first place and require effort every single day if they are going to work. Before finalising any values, review them over weeks to test the water first. Go through scenarios to make sure that they stand up within the day-to-day of your team life, and, most importantly, that you truly want to live by them. Because if you don't, you'll come unstuck. When venturing into the realms of making team values, be sure you know what you're letting yourself in for. If you're not prepared to put in the work in producing them, and to then live by them, it's actually better if you don't bother in the first place – because badly executed values can create a more toxic environment than not having any values at all.

KATE: The vision for London, GOLD, was a bold and scary goal. It was so high and lofty we absolutely needed to break it down into something more manageable. The process of developing our vision, values and behaviours took many meetings spread over a couple of months in the early part of 2010. There was a great deal of talking, listening and sharing.

It was a time-consuming and lengthy process, and necessarily so. It was vital that we heard from everybody in the group. We were a large group of players and staff, and every person's input was valid and valued. We would be prompted with questions by our psychologist, Tom Cross, and then break out into ever-changing small groups to share and discuss our thoughts. We would agree on our feedback points and share with the whole group. Back and forth. To and fro. At times it felt like we would never reach total team agreement.

The values we built to underpin the vision for London were, I would say, pretty generic. You would be able to find these in many corporate and sports team manifestos. They were the well-established traits of high-performing teams, and so it is understandable why we would push towards these words at this juncture. However generic the words may seem from the outside, we gained some level of understanding through the discussions we had, although the meaning wasn't as explicit as the values we established pre-Rio. Our values were:

Pride
Belief
Excellence
Integrity
Commitment
Unity

The length of time we spent on developing our vision, values and behaviours back in 2010 might seem like wasted time to some. When you have a deadline looming on the horizon, time is precious. However, time spent in those meeting rooms in the initial stage of our London cycle played an essential role in our eventual gold medal victory in Rio 2016.

HELEN: In contrast to the hours, weeks and months we spent on making our vision, values and behaviours (VVB) for the London Olympic cycle, in 2014, when we were deciding on our VVB for the first time in the Rio Olympic cycle, it felt like we were done and dusted within a few weeks. Coincidentally, we settled on a very similar set of words: Togetherness. Respect. Professional. Be Better. Challenge. Demand. Honesty. The whole training squad and staff were involved, the same psychologist as in 2010 led us through a process similar to what had gone before, and over the course of a handful of meetings, we established our vision and values.

However, the lack of time just didn't allow for true and honest discussions, meaning that, this time, there was about a tenth of the meaning attached to each value. Of course, there will be times when a decision needs to be made: you definitely can't keep talking without taking action for ever. But it felt as though there were a lot of things left unsaid and a lack of alignment, especially between the older players and those new into the team, through no fault of anyone. The need to 'get this done' was evident, and that's what we did – we settled. We were left with words on posters and photographs and videos on our laptops, and sadly that's where they remained.

Unfortunately, all too often the making of visions and values is viewed as a one-time event, the business, for example, of a team awayday. However, as I've already said, getting them right takes time, which gives the potential values and conversations time to breathe. How we see things in the heat of a conflict is very different from when everything is all fun and games on a team awayday. The only way to facilitate this is through giving time and space. All situations, from the average day-to-day, to the biggest pitch of your life, need to be reflected and given space in your values.

Connection brings motivation

KATE: The team values we forged in 2010 for the upcoming London Olympics were good foundational values for any team. Each of the words conveyed meaning and absolutely related to purpose. On reflection, although the words we chose were important, on some level it was the discussions that took place that had the most powerful consequences.

The depth of conversations in our small groups of six or seven, about the values, ultimately gave the words their weight. As we moved from group to group, players would talk about why certain values resonated with them and why they thought that would be an important factor in bringing our goal of 'GOLD' to life. We were a thoughtful group and were encouraged to facilitate our own small group conversations skilfully, ensuring everyone had a voice and were listened to. We were a relatively inexperienced group at senior international level. Although there were a number of players with vast experience, me being one of them, we were all encouraged to relate past successes and failures to help create our new collective identity. Younger, less experienced players were able to provide some check and challenge, ask good questions and offer a fresh new take.

Danny, our Head Coach, had bravely devolved power to the whole group; what we did mattered, what we said mattered, how we felt mattered. The hundreds of hours spent in meetings not only helped us solidify our team values but also enabled us to create meaning. We were learning a lot more about one another than perhaps we knew at the time. We were really sharing our thoughts, fears, hopes and experiences, and, in doing so, were connecting at an exceptionally deep level.

With hindsight I can see that this depth of connection to the values and to one another was probably what was lacking in 2014. I can't disagree with the values we settled on back in 2014, detailed by Helen above. On paper they read well. However, the reality of what I experienced day to day was different from this list of values. The result of this, in my opinion, was a behaviour gap in the group. If I am going to work expecting honesty because it is a team value and what I experience is a lack of transparency, over time this will likely build up layers of negative emotions and thoughts.

I have worked with a number of teams in both corporate and public settings, and one of the major issues that arises regularly is the lack of collective understanding of what lies within the team values. Through our life experiences we have all built up notions of what certain words and values mean to us. In a team setting this can cause problems when what one person believes to be a true reflection of 'professionalism' in a work setting clashes with your view of the same value. Who is 'right' and who is 'wrong' in this instance? And can the team function with disagreements on the group values and what they mean? I absolutely believe that the team can function well with slightly different takes and experiences of a team value. However, I also believe that there needs to be some honest robust conversations around agreed behaviours and habits that the whole group buys into and enacts.

I don't believe we had really discussed what underpinned our seven values back in 2014, which I think goes some way to explain exactly where I was emotionally and mentally at the time. For the majority of 2013 and early 2014 I had a sense of unease and a growing sense of foreboding. I knew that something wasn't right, but I was caught up in the daily routine and I couldn't get a grip of where the root of my issues lay. I wasn't alone in feeling disjointed and a little bit lost during this time.

I didn't know what I was challenging myself or my teammates against. Our values were, in effect, hollow.

HELEN: They were hollow values because we didn't use them to navigate direction or processes. If you've decided that these values are what you want to live by, they're important to you, so weave them into everything you do, every policy. Recruitment, reviews, bonuses, meetings, dismissals and so on. From the first contact an employee or customer has with a company these values form the basis of everything, and that needs to come across. Our psychologist, Tom Cross, made this happen during the London cycle. His prompts and challenges reminded us of what we'd signed up to. I'm sure at times he felt like the 'bad cop', but he was right to do what he did, and that's why we were able to create the team environment that we did in London.

It was the same in 2015, and, again, bringing our values off the page was fundamental to our success. Time was of the essence, and so once again we incorporated them into all the processes discussed above, but this time we created a VVB that was so memorable it reverberated round everything we did. Our vision for London, 'GOLD', was so impactful, almost to the point it created its own value and elicited the required behaviours. But in 2015 the group worked tirelessly and used the experiences of 2014 to fuel the emotions and appreciate what was now needed to get back on track. With these things in mind we created the following unique values:

We Are One Team.
We Are Winners.
Be Alive.

We'd never had anything like it before. Our discussions were emotive, passionate, honest and from the heart. Most, if not all, of us lived wholeheartedly in those meetings, and by opening ourselves up, by sharing our true reflections, we created values that would 'be the difference'. They were, in some ways, aspirational values, and they needed to be. We weren't doing or being these things currently. The words we used created meaning; it was practically dripping from every word. It was in our language. We owned them, meaning we would use them. They were simple, clear, meaningful and memorable. Everyone knew where they stood and what we needed to do. Together.

We Are One Team

HELEN: This came from a place where, if we were totally honest with ourselves, wasn't a particularly nice place to be. We were so far away from being a team, so this value was imperative. Like the rebuilding of any relationship, we had to grow back together and work hard on regaining trust. Actively displaying our togetherness would therefore be vital. We also needed to value every single person's contribution. The strength of our team was about everyone.

KATE: People might have got fed up with me asking people to make sure they were in the right team kit over the years; I was a stickler for it. I had been well schooled in my early years at Hightown Hockey Club that what you wore in a team mattered because it helped form the story you told about yourselves and the story that other people believed. A team who all wear the same kit look together, strong, proud and defiant. We all needed to be very mindful that Home Nations kit was kept for Home Nations training, and GB kit was the only thing we wore when we were all together as a collective. It's such a small thing and can seem a bit nit-picky, but it is these small details that make up a truly cohesive team.

We Are Winners

HELEN: For me, having this value created the difference between bronze in London and gold in Rio. We didn't shy away from any difficult conversations; we were prepared to face them head on, and this was one of those conversations. We knew deep down that we didn't know how to win. We didn't talk about it or celebrate it enough for the fear of hurting someone's feelings. We needed to be ruthless while remaining respectful and humble. When Kate and I first got into the senior team, if, before a match, an individual player was celebrating a milestone, such as a hundred international caps, someone would always say, 'We never win on a milestone.' I couldn't quite believe what I was hearing – a negative self-fulfilling prophecy if ever I heard one! Thankfully, we had at least eliminated this kind of talk in the London cycle, but, still, we needed to take it up a notch.

'We'll win this game over 70 minutes, and if we're losing with only a few minutes on the clock, we *will* get another chance.' Chris Mayer, my club coach at Leicester, said this before playing a big game in the Premier League, and it stuck with me for ever. It's perfect. First, you have to believe you'll make a chance, but, most importantly, you have to be in the right mindset to take it. Big matches are rarely won by more than one goal. It's rarely going to be about outplaying an opponent when the margins are so fine. Therefore, in order to win the Premier League, a World Cup or an Olympic Games, you have to know how to win when it's tight, when the game can go either way. And you have to have practised week after week, day after day. Personally, I couldn't stand losing one little bit. It would piss me off so much I could barely speak afterwards. I would struggle to look people in the eye – that's how much it annoyed me. But if you let those emotions creep in before the final whistle, you've already lost. So, we learned to deal with that uncomfortable feeling. Every session it was on our minds but especially on 'Thinking Thursday', which we'll look at in detail in Chapter 4, on processes. It was all about practising to stay in the moment right until the last second. Teams *can* learn that – that's exactly what 'Fergie time' meant for the Manchester United men's football team. So, we learned it. We literally taught ourselves how to 'find a way to win'.

Be Alive

HELEN: This value was everything for me. I'm not sure if there was a tinge of desperation on my part, but when we were going through this process all I kept thinking was: 'What's the point of any of this if we aren't going to give our all?' I couldn't stop thinking about people's eyes. Everything is in the eyes. You're either there, present and engaged, or you're not. We'd wasted two and a half years already, we had only 18 months left; we had to make every session count.

KATE: 'Ball pace!' A player's knee-jerk response to a coach's question echoed around the makeshift meeting room in a warm Barcelona hotel bedroom back in 2003. In the team we would call this a 'buzzword bingo' answer, something you can say when you're not sure of what to say or you hadn't been listening to the question. It was chancy but you might just get away with it. Unfortunately for this player in question, we had been talking about defending and so there was no ball to have any pace! It is easy to let your mind drift in meetings; we've all done it. But the more present we are the better we can question, act and bring to life whatever is being discussed. When we are alive we are respecting the people around us and ourselves.

HELEN: These values were so authentic, unique and true to us. I loved them and still do. Going through the process of writing about them now still brings out the same passion in me as I had in 2015. No other person, sports team or company in the world has these values – how inspiring is it to know that? Don't be afraid to get creative, be yourself, think outside of the box. There's absolutely nothing wrong with generic words as values, but instead of fading into the background, why not use your values to sell yourself and leverage on what makes you different? By using words that reflect who you are, and how you want to come across, this is your chance to be truly authentic.

Take ownership

KATE: Unique and authentic values are also more sticky! We humans have only so much storage space in our brains, and so we filter what stays in and what can be left out and forgotten. Our brains have learned to reject the unnecessary and keep what matters. If your team values really mean something to you and your teammates, they are far more likely to stay front of mind and positively influence your decision-making processes.

Team processes are a powerful way to ensure your values become more than just semantics. We love processes so much we have dedicated a whole chapter to them! When designing a way to support the return of an experienced player back to the team, we leant on our values and created our Welcome Ceremony. We go into this in some detail in Chapter 4, but, in short, part of the ceremony involved three players voluntarily taking a team value and sharing what this value meant to the team and themselves more personally. This was incredibly compelling and further embedded our values into the group.

HELEN: Kate and I are thankful that we, as a whole squad, had an element of control over the whole process of change when going from part-time to full-time training, and throughout the formulation of our VVB. This allowed us to consider, and really *own*, the meaning of every word as we went along. We appreciate that, for most companies and schools – or any organisation for that matter – this would be quite a rarity and potentially an unrealistic aim.

If we're saying that an organisation's values should reflect the fabric of what and who it wants to be about, it is inevitable that company values will be imposed on employees from above, rather than employees being able to develop and drive them themselves. New employees will, of course, be joining teams and departments as well, but that doesn't mean those values can't have the same impact. Even in large companies there are always smaller groups of people that create teams in their own right. In these instances, it is possible and highly advisable to work through the values as a smaller team and create your own meaning about how they can work for you. Of course, they need to reflect and contribute to the company values and vision, but it is also possible to make them authentic to you, and the energy of your team. As mentioned above, if companies are hiring new employees with their values at the heart of those appointments, this process will be even easier.

KATE: I think it would be fair to say that some team values resonate with some people more than others. It's a natural occurrence in all teams because we're different. Perhaps one of your team values also happens to be one of your personal values that you live your life by and therefore has a deeper meaning for you. It could be that you have a strong affiliation with a value because of research you've done. We all have our own complex set of thoughts and opinions based on our personalities and previous life experiences.

My personal bias for almost anything in life, values included, is towards anything that conveys emotion in me. Personal and unique values really speak to me and the person that I am. Of course, generic terms are just as worthy as uncommon values in terms of the impact they can have on team performance. As long as the words are authentic to the group, the meaning is understood and they have been bought into, any words can work. As an individual in that team, really it is on me to know my bias and to work with that bias to make that value work for me personally. Values are what the team and the people in those teams make of them.

The future

KATE: Our understanding of how we align with values and what they mean to us is more prevalent than ever. Human beings around the globe are increasingly making decisions based on their summations of a group's values. We want to work for employers who we know have a shared view of what is important to us. We are far more likely to invest time, money and energy into people and companies that work in synergy with who we want to be and how we want to live. Leaders must role-model their team values, repeat them and live by them. To avoid cynicism around values, leaders must be about the values every day, both in thoughts and in actions.

Now more than ever we want certainty and credibility from our leaders. Knowledge is power, and as we arm ourselves with a deeper insight into companies, groups and organisations it is only the truly authentic that will survive. The next generation of employees and consumers will demand to see genuine ownership of deep-rooted core values and visions. As the human race evolves, the need to connect your values to who you are and how you want to be remembered will be a matter of survival. In a fast-paced, polarised and uncertain world, we will more readily associate ourselves with those that hold similar values to our own. So, be mindful of your values, understand how they sit with your moral compass and your potential impact on your team and society as a whole.

Team values have become quite the hot topic now and rightly so. In a globalised information-sharing space we have more opportunities than ever to enlighten and educate ourselves. We are being encouraged to explore our own sense of self and our place in the world more than ever. We care more about what values our employers, retailers and businesses live by. We want to align ourselves with like-minded products and people.

Generic or unique, many or few, values work as essential 'whats' to your 'whys' when they are understood and owned by you and your team. We believe that the time and importance you place on your team values directly correlates with your team engagement and success. These words should be everywhere in actions and thoughts. They can serve as poignant reminders, cornerstones for challenge and as tools in recruitment.

The only thing to avoid at all costs is hollow values. Those values that look great in a slide deck but mean very little in real life are not worth anyone's time or energy. Values that hold no significant meaning to the group as a whole will likely do little to help the team or company reach its vision or goal. Heed our hard-earned lesson and spend some time talking about your team values with your teammates or colleagues. This time well spent will ensure a shared understanding and joined-up sense of purpose. In order to challenge yourself and your teammates fully, you'll need to go one step farther and be explicit about the behaviours that underpin your values. In the next chapter we will share how we made our values live and breathe.

Team huddle

Team values are an important part of any team culture. It is vital that your team gives time to the formation of your values as the discussions alone will help create a unified understanding which in turn will form bonds of trust and respect. Your values will ideally help support your collective vision and bring it off the page and into reality. If your team's values are already established, there is still a lot to be gained from talking about how you connect to the values and what impact they bring.

Questions to consider

- What do you need to be about as a team in order for your vision to be realised?
- What are must-have values for your team to flourish?
- How do you want to be perceived internally and externally?
- What kind of team do you all want to belong to?
- Have you taken the time to really consider what the team values mean to you personally?
- Do you understand what they mean to your teammates?
- Are your team values generic or unique? Either way, do you know what they mean for your team?

Key team tactics

- The greatest gift you can give your team is time on your team values. Whether you are starting with a blank page or taking ownership of already-existing company values, the more open the conversation is the better the connection.
- Creating a safe space for everyone to contribute is vital to ensure you get the most from your open and honest conversations. Encourage debate and discussion.

Facilitate good active listening. This can be practised by having one person speak on a topic for a period of time and their partner or other group members listening to hear and not merely listening to respond.

- Take personal and collective ownership and responsibility for making the team values come off the page. Leaders must own them, demonstrate them and drive them. Weave the words into your daily actions and processes to make them live and breathe.
- Make your values 'sticky' by making connections and discussing meaning. Clarify the meaning of the words you use as your team values. Try not to assume anything!
- Checking in and challenging the team values regularly will help you celebrate progress and know where to tweak for improvement. Enjoy the never-ending pursuit of excellence.

3

Team behaviours

We believe that we were our most successful, as a team and as individuals, when we had been encouraged to examine our collective behaviours. Agreed team behaviours enable us to feel connected and safe and fulfil a basic human need of belonging. The small moments of physical, verbal and non-verbal communication between teammates produce powerful team dynamics and a winning chemistry. You can see it, hear it and feel it.

If your vision is your 'why', your values are your 'what', then your team behaviours are your 'how'. In our experience, when these three fundamental elements of team culture are aligned, led from the top and driven from within, team performance excels. We hear a lot about corporate visions and company values, but how often are we privy to the intricate details of daily behaviours? Visions and values are, of course, imperative – that's why we have dedicated two chapters to them – but without action those words are exactly that, just words.

In this chapter we will demonstrate how agreed team behaviours were critical to our team success and were in fact our 'winning difference'. We will detail the importance of in-depth honest conversations and what those conversations ultimately enabled us to do as a team. In doing so, we hope to press home to you that with this key level of joined-up thinking, your team can shift from good to great and reach your ultimate goal with authenticity and togetherness.

The winning difference

HELEN: We'd been in Rio 21 days, and up until that point I'd completely resisted the temptation to read any articles or anything to do with hockey the entire time. It's not something I tend to do anyway, but as a team we had signed off social media for the duration of the Games, meaning I was barely on my phone. The one app I did regularly look at, though, was BBC Sport – to stay up to date with the Olympics, what to watch on my rest days, and, of course, to check how pretty Team GB was sitting in the medal table.

It was in the morning after beating Spain 3–1 in the quarter-final when this headline on the live feed caught my eye: 'They are the epitome of what a sports team should be.' Colin Murray spoke about how he had been following our team from the first match and that he'd been enthralled by the team's performances, attitudes and togetherness. As I read this, it felt for the first time as though someone in the media truly understood what we were about. He completely and utterly grasped the importance of *us*, the team, and the impact our togetherness had on everything. I continued to read, half expecting to see a 'star' name or top goal scorer singled out, as so often happens, but he didn't. He spoke only about the team, all of us. He got it. He got us. That made me so proud because it hadn't been easy to get to that point, far from it.

In fact, to get to that point I think is one of the hardest things a team can achieve, because it takes constant effort every single day. We didn't just *have* our values, we *were* our values, and Colin could see, hear and feel them being played out through every behaviour. We brought them off the page. So many companies and organisations have fantastic visions and values that sometimes really do inspire. But they don't always translate into everyday action. This is where your team can be the difference and can really stand out from the crowd by delivering on your vision and values, and that is achieved in how you behave.

KATE: We had talked about behaviours before in previous teams, before our centralised programme. But for a number of reasons those conversations just didn't have the same impact. The first time a group discussion on behaviours made a real meaningful impression was in 2010, in our culture-building meetings which we detailed in the previous two chapters. The increase in National Lottery funding bought us the luxury of time. We could have used those extra hours in our centralised programme to train more regularly on the hockey pitch or lift more weights. And while those aspects of our training did increase, we all bought into the fact that time well spent on our culture would reap rewards in the long run. We needed to be on the same page to be able to navigate ourselves collectively through high-pressure chaotic environments.

When I look at all of the international squads I have had the privilege of playing in, I cast my eyes over many world-class players. I have played alongside and trained with some of the best players in the world. As good as these players were, we didn't have enough 'stars' to win games for us consistently; I'm not sure any team does. For the experienced players among the group back in 2010 we knew that, if we wanted to achieve our vision of 'GOLD', it was going to require a complete squad effort, not just the 11 on the field or the 16/18 on the match sheet; this was a whole training squad and staff endeavour. Every single person, every single day.

I have many memories of this team ethos in action. One of my fondest and clearest examples of our culture being played out happened in a training session on the London Olympic turf long before the Olympic branding had been put up or a game had been played. We had home advantage and trained on the field as soon as it was laid. In the beginning it was nothing more than a building site with a couple of bright blue pitches with electric-pink surrounds. We trained there almost every week, as the stadium slowly rose from the ground, and the pitch became an arena. It was a visual reminder of what awaited the final selected 16. This one session on that turf took place just a couple of weeks before the first ball would be played at the London Games, and the whole squad was still present even though selection had already been done. Dreams had been made and hearts had been broken, and yet here we all were.

Twenty-six bodies lay on the floor just over the baseline, on the luminous pink surround of the newly laid blue 'Smurf turf'. 'Get up!' Dave, our strength and conditioning coach, shouted. 'You're going again.' I dragged my tired body off the floor. I was breathing hard, gasping for air. We'd never run this many shuttles before; the final number had been kept from us. We were to run until they said stop. As I turned around to face the next shuttle run which lay out ahead of me, I looked along the row of people to my right. I saw friends and teammates in pain, staggering up to get their toe behind the baseline. What struck me in that moment was that we were just a few weeks away from the opening game of the London 2012 Olympic Games. On this very pitch on which we were running now, I and 15 other members of this squad would soon face Japan and ten of these women would not. Those ten were mentally and emotionally devastated, having just missed out on selection. And yet, here they were, running alongside me, pushing themselves beyond their limit, and pushing me to be better, do better. I have a photograph of us all together after this session, sweaty and exhausted. It remains one of my most treasured possessions.

Accountability

HELEN: The actual process of determining team behaviours, over the course of establishing our vision, values and behaviours (VVB) was probably the hardest part of all. Kate and I have worked with corporate teams and school pupils since Rio, and it is clear that the ability to get to an actual behaviour is the tricky part. Our team was no different, especially in 2010. So when you try to operationalise your values into behaviours with your team, be patient with yourselves; it's not an easy thing to do. To help the process, keep asking yourselves, 'What does that look like?' or 'What would we see?' If we came into your place of work, your school or even your home and asked, 'What are we going to see, hear and feel from every person we meet and every room we walk into?' would you know? Would you be able to formulate a list? When our team started deliberating this in our small group circles and then feeding back into our big group circle, we had reams and reams of behaviours – too many to list and too many to remember. 'Can I please refer you to Article 25, point two, paragraph three, section C?'! This might be exactly what your team needs, but that wasn't us at that time, nor necessary. So, to keep things open, short, succinct and precise, we simply established two main behaviours we all thought summed it all up:

> Have intent.
> Feedback (a) Support ourselves first, then each other.
>   (b) Challenge ourselves first, then each other.

The responsibility was with each of us, and the team was always front of mind. Every day we would ask ourselves and challenge ourselves against our team standards. 'Would a gold medallist eat that for breakfast, Helen? Hmm, maybe not, well then let's change the breakfast.' If anyone wasn't sure what they should be eating for breakfast, then they were encouraged to proactively use the expertise around them – make an appointment with our nutritionist, for example, and make a plan. From how much weight we were lifting in the gym, to the number of hours of sleep we were getting at night, to the choice of kit we wore to training – everything had a consequence and everything had to be thought about. This was a constantly evolving beast, and, in the end, because our vision was so impactful, many of the squad referred to our behaviours as our 'gold medal standards'.

This didn't just fall on the captain's shoulders or the leadership group who had been voted in specifically to lead the team on our VVB. This was about every person. In *your* team, this is about every person. It has to be constant, and at times we found it exhausting. Living up to those gold medal standards on a daily basis was challenging. There were plenty of times when we wanted to give in to the devil on our shoulder. The voice that appears in your head telling you to just stop during a running session or has you gazing out of the window in a team meeting. But most of us had a much louder voice in our heads that could often overpower any other – that sense of being a good teammate. You might not be doing a running session, but whichever team you're in, every action you make affects the people around you, either positively or negatively. Like you, if I make a bad choice, I would be letting my teammates down. It may sound a bit trite, but we took our role of setting an example very seriously. To do anything less is selfish, and to win gold, or to achieve the vision your team has committed to, you need to be selfless.

Within a matter of months we started to see the difference this was making and the potential we could realise. We won our first medal on a world stage, albeit as England at the Champions Trophy, a tournament for the top six nations in the world in 2010. This was backed up by another bronze medal at the World Cup six weeks later. These kinds of outcomes are obviously important, but they don't tell the whole story. Just because results are good it doesn't mean your behaviours are right, or that they can't be better.

Key performance indicators (KPIs) play a role in providing feedback on whether your behaviours are doing what you want them to. For us, these were things like the number of times we possessed the ball in the opposition circle, or penalty corner conversion rates – if these were a certain percentage, they tended to lead to a win. In business KPIs might include attrition rates, or for schools it could be pupil attendance rates. All of these things add to the story, but for me it can sometimes come down to a feeling. While match wins, profit made or exam grades are how we are all judged externally, what we feel is just as important. That can't always be measured, but it's absolutely worth taking note of. For example, increased levels of engagement, interaction, or even eye contact from pupils, would surely give a great feeling to any teacher. The results we had helped bring clarity to the changes we were making, but *feeling* like we were creating the right environment for us was just as crucial.

When you're discussing your behaviours, it's important to remember that every team is unique – what works for one team is unlikely to work for another – and in 2015 we were in a completely different place as a team and as people. With retirements and changes in personnel, our experience and maturity levels were very different. The challenges of 2014 also gave us a lot of baggage to wade through and clear out. As ever, we sat, we talked and we debated. We considered lots of behaviours we felt would really bring each value to life. They were carved out through time together, through discussion. By challenging ourselves and with bravery we acknowledged the lack of trust and the need to rebuild that trust. This disparity meant that the specifics of behaviour statements, which we'd said no to in 2010, were now potentially the best thing we could have. These lists were the real nitty-gritty of each one of our values and the essence of who we were as a group and where we wanted to go.

Our behaviour statements

We Are One Team
We respect each other

We accept differences
    It's OK to listen
        You don't always have to talk

We belong to one team

I've got your back
And
You've got mine

We stand in this bubble together

Belong now   Belong forever

There is no bullshit

And

There are no excuses
I am connected to you
    We wear the same kit
        We are tight
            We talk to each other
                We share with each other

We stamp out fires early
Talk to me
Listen to me

We share the load   Together we have strength

We are one team.

We Are Winners
I ask myself
  What can I do to be a winner?
    What will I do to be a winner?
And then I ask you

I fight for the team
  I am first to everything
    I am aggressive
      I don't jump
        I don't turn my back
          Nothing goes through me

I never give up

We never give up

I persevere – I find a way – I make it work – I solve the problem – I adapt

We play smart – We train smart

I win my battles on the field
And
I help you win yours

We all possess a winning attitude
  We celebrate together
    We do the right thing
      And we do it with conviction
      We play as we train
        We push ourselves in every session

We listen to the experts and drive our standards ever higher

I don't lie to myself

I am honest
I am a winner
We are winners.

Be Alive
I'm alive
I'm engaged
    I'm listening
        I'm contributing
           I respond

I'm on it
I'm in it

My eyes

I look at people when they're talking

I look around the pitch when I'm playing

My body language has tone and is ready
I'm learning

I'm asking questions
    I use the coaches
        I look at the video
           I talk to my teammates

I learn from myself

I reply to e-mails and I fill in forms

I'm on time

I'm prepared

I leave my outside shit at the gate

I know myself and I support you being yourself

I know when to switch off

I'm Alive.

HELEN: Our behaviours covered everything on and off the pitch. When you saw us celebrate every goal in a tight bunch all together in Rio, that's because it's there in our 'We Are Winners' behaviour statement: 'We celebrate together.' You might think this is a given for a sports team, but it's not. When you heard us repeat in interviews the importance of the whole squad of 31, we did so because it's part of 'We Are One Team' in the line 'Together we have strength'. There is also some pretty mundane stuff in those statements as well! It can't all be hard-hitting emotive stuff, you know. One such statement was: 'I reply to emails and I fill in forms'. That kind of thing is hardly going to set the world alight or get you hyped up for a big game! It's not likely to come out in a team huddle, for example. But how many of you are waiting for a response to an email so you can get on with parts of your job? Imagine how efficient you could become if these types of behaviours became the norm in your team. It's these small details when you add them all together that in the end really make the difference, and they did for us.

The combination of the behaviour statements of these three values culminated in what Colin, and thousands, if not millions, saw when they watched us in Rio. We did this in Rio, because it's what we had been doing everyday of our life in the centralised programme. Thirty-one women doing their job, playing their role. Doing what we'd signed up to do. It's all there, written down in our behaviour statements. And these weren't just words on a page; they were us. We came up with those words, and we all collectively brought them to life.

KATE: Once we had spent time really unpacking what our team values meant in relation to our team behaviours, it made decision making much clearer. As an individual, you know either exactly or principally what you are challenging yourself against. You also know what all of your teammates are holding themselves to and what you can challenge them against. In order to have that level of trust, that everybody in the group is doing the right thing for the team, everybody in the team needs to know what is expected of them. When you don't know what you're signing up to, it's impossible to know what you're challenging yourself and your teammates against.

The fact that we were all accountable for our culture helped us navigate the hugely pressurised environment of elite sport. We will talk about selection in more detail in the coming chapters. However, to know that every day you are going to give all of yourself for the good of the team and that you yourself may not benefit or be selected come the Olympics is a harsh reality. We were a team, a collective unit, all driving each other in the same direction towards our team vision. And yet, we were also in direct competition with one another. It was high pressure and high emotion. Our team behaviours could never take any of this away. To a large extent we wouldn't want it to. What they did, though, was give us focus, something to lock on to and grip hold of. Centring your attention on tasks and behaviours will help you be mindful, be present and help you cope with the daily pressure of being in a high-performing team striving for excellence – hence the importance of ensuring that all viewpoints were welcomed and all ideas discussed.

And while our culture pre-London and in the final run-up to Rio was absolutely about everybody equally, if the critical mass in the squad hadn't role-modelled the agreed team behaviours, it just wouldn't have worked. When Malcolm Gladwell, in his book *The Tipping Point: How Little Things Can Make a Big Difference*, talks about messages and behaviours spreading like viruses do, this absolutely describes team culture at its best. There is certainly a need for designated leaders to lead by example, whether they be members of the board or section managers. Importantly, though, the culture will never work unless a larger group of 'unassigned' leaders also exemplify the team's vision, values and behaviours. It is these team members that ensure that you have a critical mass of people leading on the behaviours and making those behaviours spread like a contagion. In our environment, it might be that a few players start bringing their protein shake to the gym and then, before you know it, everyone has one with them. This was the power of our behaviours at their very best. In your corporate environment, it might be that when the leader closes their laptop in an in-person meeting then all laptops begin to be closed more regularly. An example in a school could see Year 11 pupils being diligent about putting their litter in the bin after break time and all other year groups following suit over time. Everyone is accountable, and everyone is playing a role.

A note of caution

HELEN: There are, as with anything, potential problems that could arise when formulating a list of behaviours. One of them is knowing when to stop! However, it's also incredibly important to get down to some specific detail, which the depth of our discussions really allowed for. I can't stress how important these conversations are. Take our behaviour statement 'I'm on time'. It seems obvious what this means, right? But if you were to ask several people in your team what 'being on time' means to them, I bet you'd get a few different answers. For some, getting somewhere five to ten minutes early means being on time. For others, being ready to start at the allotted time will suffice, and some think arriving just as the clock ticks to the exact time is good enough. Then there are those who actually think it's OK to be late, and to them that is their 'on time'! Now, you might think this is nit-picking, and brought up in a certain way at certain times this would be true. However, the conversation and agreement about what the group accepts as 'on time' saves a thousand little moments of frustration and annoyance. It also helps prevent people from feeling constantly judged and on the outside of the team. Those small seemingly insignificant moments build up, layer upon layer, over time and can cause huge damage to people, relationships within the team, and team outcome. Once everyone knows where they stand, the ability to challenge, and support each other becomes so much easier.

KATE: When considering team behaviours, it is vital that your team distinguishes between 'bullshit' and reality. As an example, in the process of discussing the behaviours for our team value 'Be Alive' one player put forward the idea that we shouldn't allow grumpiness, and that we should all arrive at training with a smile on our face. This one statement sparked a brilliant conversation in the group. What transpired was an increased focus on awareness of our personal energy levels, and on what we were either giving or taking from the group. We felt it was unrealistic to have a robotic control over our state of mind and always arrive at training with beaming smiles and bouncy energy levels. However, we could be mindful of where we were emotionally and consider what impact we might be having on our own and our teammates' performance.

There are a few great takeaways from this example, the most important one being that it is imperative that everything is grounded in the team's day-to-day reality. Of course, team behaviours will, at times, be challenging and not come easy to team members or the team. However, there needs to be a healthy dose of sense and sensibility in the formation of any such behaviour lists. The second point to note here is that all viewpoints were valid and every idea welcomed. The conversation about mental state and managing energy levels might never have occurred had it not been for that one player bravely inputting her thoughts to the group. One of the problems with team behaviours, then, can be formulating them around an idealistic view of what should be, rather than what can be. But a potentially even more challenging issue might be when those differing views about behaviours cannot be raised or discussed at all. Conversation brings clarity to team behaviours and should be encouraged in your team at all times.

Challenging from compassion not judgement

HELEN: Once clarity is established, it's easier not only to challenge but to support the people in your team. When you get to know each other really well, if any behaviour is out of the ordinary then it is much easier to spot. This was the case for us, and it was necessary because we didn't get it right all the time. None of us came to our training base, Bisham Abbey, fully energised and raring to go every day. At times, we were late, some of us didn't wear the right kit, we weren't 'alive' and we made mistakes – thousands of them. The understanding of that was built in, and so checking in with teammates became something of the norm. Not just for me but for all of us. We made a concerted effort to assume good intentions. Whenever somebody didn't live up to our behaviour statements, we would first ask whether everything was OK before anything else. We were careful to make sure our expectations were realistic, and by building in the means for individuality and mistakes, we allowed for the fact that we are all humans and we would never do everything right all of the time. This might take a complete shift in mindset; it did a little for me if I'm honest. And it might also start with remembering that you're human, too, and you make mistakes as well, and that's OK.

KATE: We can all slip up from time to time and may well welcome a timely reminder of what is expected of us. Ideally, team behaviours are used as a positive proactive resource to check, challenge and maintain collective forward momentum. We were by no means perfect, and as a group we had a very fortunate and timely admonishment of the importance of our behaviours at the Champions Trophy in 2016. It was a tricky time as we'd had selection for the Olympics and we were just six weeks away from Rio. Some old sketchy behaviours started rearing their ugly heads during the tournament, so it was red flashing lights and warning siren time for the leadership team – for myself, Helen and Alex Danson. We had won only the last match out of six at that tournament. Whether results were relevant or not, we knew the importance of group values and behaviours, having seen what could happen to a team's culture in such a short space of time between 2012 and 2014.

This lack of focus and attention to detail on our culture could absolutely have been our downfall in Rio, and therefore it had to be addressed as soon as possible. With the help of Danny and the team psychologist, Andrea Furst, we did just that. We went to Rio having reviewed our vision, values and behaviours as a collective, made any tweaks we felt necessary, and determined to be vigilant to any future warning signs. Team values that are underpinned by agreed team behaviours or unwritten 'rules' can have a massive psychological edge on team performance. This is particularly prevalent when there is an increased sense of urgency and pressure to perform. Having the ability to be present enough to look at a team's behaviours with a critical eye at all points in your journey will ensure that culture thrives and excellence is achieved.

A connective force

HELEN: Most significantly of all, our behaviour statements got us to the holy grail, the ability to not just cope under pressure but to thrive when the pressure was most potent. The more you repeat expected behaviours, the more instinctive they become. In doing that, it creates habits, which means, come the high-pressure situation of an Olympic Games, for example, when you literally have one shot to make it count, you don't have to think about anything other than doing what you'd been doing every day. You don't have to think anything different. In fact, the best thing you can do is to not change anything. When faced with pressure, delusions of grandeur can have an impact for some; for others the opposite is true. Either way, it's so easy to go off script, but all your team really needs is for you to stick to the agreed behaviours. That's the only thing your team is expecting. If you try to do anything other than that, it can actually be very off-putting for the rest of your team. One person trying to be the hero, trying to do everything when the pressure is on, is not very helpful at all!

If you'd watched our first game of the Rio Olympics, when the half-time whistle blew, you would have seen us all, without hesitation, run into the changing room, past the Australians trudging in after a very hard, physical first half. This wasn't coincidence; this was a behaviour we had done for months in training matches in the lead-up. In those matches, when it was freezing cold, when I was tired and had the remnants of training fatigue in my legs, I didn't always see the point of doing it. But, during that first match, when I set off to the changing room I experienced a jolt of adrenaline I just wasn't expecting, and I know that some of my teammates also experienced that same rush of energy. It was such a simple behaviour, something anyone could do, and yet the outcome it elicited was more powerful than anyone could ever have imagined, just when we needed it most.

At their very best, team behaviours are a connective force transmitting positive energy between groups of people. Although this might not immediately appear to translate to a corporate setting, if you exchange running into the changing room at half-time with saying 'hello' and making eye contact with your colleagues each day, the outcome could well be the same. What your equivalent is, of course, will be up to you and your team, but taking time on this aspect will have a big impact when it matters most.

In our experience of playing in elite sports teams and working with large corporate teams, behaviours are a key element to exceptional team culture. They are often the last area of a team's culture to be addressed, given the least time and yet they have the potential to have the biggest impact on performance. It's all too easy to assume that we all know what the team values mean for us behaviourally and that we are all on the same page. We all know what 'assume' means in a team context! It makes a proverbial ass out of 'u' and 'me'.

By being open to honest discussions about behaviours at an overarching level we get connectivity between team members and with the team values and vision. Connectivity leads to better working relationships, more respect, increased challenge and support, and better outcomes.

Behaviour statements worked for us in the lead-up to Rio because we had lost our way behaviourally. We needed to have an explicit shared understanding to enable us to turn things around very quickly. Equally, having a broader behavioural prompt such as 'gold medal standards' worked brilliantly for the group in the lead-up to London. Behaviours are very personal to your group. How you choose to weave them into the fabric of your team is up to you. Use them, lean on them and bring them off the page.

Establishing behaviours and principles in your company or team will give you a foundation upon which to review past outcomes. They will also help you shape your now, and, by including them in your recruitment strategies, will shape your future successes. Opportunities to see, hear and feel how values are operationalised into team behaviours by current and future employees will improve team effectiveness and sense of belonging. In this way, you will also have the ability to assess individual behavioural habits and see how they align with company culture. The collective power of team behaviours is a positive force for individuals and the team itself. We will now turn our attention to the steps we put in place to allow our environment to foster the behaviours we had set out to deliver.

Team huddle

Discussing your team behaviours might be challenging for a number of reasons. Behaviours are the way you act and interact with others around you. It is likely that there will be a lot of personal emotion attached to your behaviours and those of your teammates. Being mindful of this fact will help you and your team navigate these conversations skilfully.

Questions to consider

- If we were to come into your place of work, what would we see, hear and feel? Would we be able to know what you and your team is about from stepping into the workspace and from our very first conversation with one of your colleagues?
- Can you think of an instance that validated who you are as a team and demonstrated what you are about?
- Are you leading on your team behaviours?
- If you are setting a good example, where have you seen this spark good energy in the team?
- How easy is it to challenge your own behaviour and that of your teammates?
- Do you know what you are measuring yourself and your teammates against?
- Are you able to use your knowledge of your team behaviours proactively and reactively?

Key team tactics

- Begin with one team value and brainstorm any actions you think you need to see in your team to bring this value to life. Depending on the size of your team, breaking into and rotating around smaller groups allows for free-flowing input from all team members.

- Create your own 'rules of engagement' for these discussions. Consider how you talk, listen and converse to get the best from everyone in the group. Practise being a good listener.
- Lists of actions are good: even the discussions about the specifics of listed actions will take you from good to great. Be specific and consider what particular actions are relevant and pertinent to your team.
- Be mindful of your energy and its effect on yourself and others. Find innovative and creative ways to document and celebrate positive behaviours demonstrated by team members. These could give you a great platform to engage in conversations around team behaviours.

4

Processes

Processes play an important role in supporting an organisational culture, helping lift behaviours off the pages of your notebooks and into the hearts and minds of your teams. The first and definitive factor of a process is that it feeds directly into a defined goal. Team processes need to be aligned to the team vision, and be built around the people and the specific context for that team. In high-pressure and/or uncertain environments, processes provide an understanding of what is required and from whom. Importantly, they help formulate clarity of roles so that actions can be performed consistently and at a high standard. They also provide various platforms for behaviours to be demonstrated and shown by everyone, which will ultimately help the team succeed in the vision. In a nutshell, processes will help your team get stuff done!

The processes that evolved for our team provided steps that needed to be taken in order to make things as good and as efficient as possible. We could not have a process for every eventuality, but what we could do was control the controllables and consider what were the known 'critical moments'. Processes also provide a framework for unknown situations, building up ideas and principles against which you and your team can align yourselves no matter how random the circumstance.

Processes also provide moments in time for vital retrospective reflection. One of the best things about having defined processes is that they can be deconstructed, allowing a clearer view of the current state of play. You are much more able to see what worked well and what didn't work so well, and make changes accordingly. All of this aids learning and growth in the wake of every success and every failure.

Supporting values and behaviours

HELEN: This may sound obvious, but the processes you create must support the values and behaviours you're wanting to live by. When the inspiration from creating a vision has started to wear off, and achieving that vision seems like months, or even years, away, it's easy to get side-tracked in the middle bit. The middle bit is the daily grind. It can't be avoided. To get to where you want to get you have to go through the sticky mess that is the middle. Acknowledging this helps, but so do your processes.

Lots of our behaviours are hockey specific and so can't be transferred exactly into your environment, unless you're a sports team, of course. However, from my experience, a lack of or poor communication is more often than not the reason for poor culture, and whatever industry you're in, learning how to make your employees feel heard and valued has to be a target for any employer. Providing space for open conversation, where players could feel safe to share their honest thoughts, feelings and ideas, as well as listen to others was a conscious process we put in place to facilitate our behaviour statements 'Talk to me, listen to me' and, most significantly, 'Stamp out fires early'. In order to do this we had various types of meetings: leadership group meetings, players and staff meetings, leadership group and staff meetings, just player meetings and also buddy group meetings, each playing a part in delivering on specific areas of our vision, values and behaviours (VVB).

For some readers, I'm sure that just the thought of all those meetings would send a shudder down the spine. There would often be the odd sigh at the end of a pitch session when I'd remind people that we had a quick players meeting, and finding times when everyone was available was, well, challenging! But I didn't mind being that person, because these meetings were the fundamental processes that kept us connected and communicating. No one wants or has time for meetings for meetings' sake, but if you frame them through the lens of a process that allows you to live your values and behaviours, then it will make them more meaningful, nurturing greater engagement from all.

The variety of meetings, facilitated by repeated process execution, also allowed us to be true to our behaviour statements 'We accept differences' and 'It's OK to listen, you don't always have to talk'. Not everyone is comfortable speaking up in large groups, or with certain people around. This isn't a bad thing and shouldn't be treated as such. But if you are to truly value everyone, spaces need to be created where everyone feels comfortable to voice their opinions. Our buddy groups, each one led by one member of the Leadership Group, were designed for this, allowing every voice to be heard.

KATE: When the pressure is on, it's really easy to neglect your behaviours. But consistency is key. The behaviour 'We stamp out fires early' was so important to me. We had all experienced first-hand post London, and in other squads, what can happen when you let the tiny sparks of disagreement and discontent go unaired. Under the pressure of our environment and the added stress of selection and major tournaments, those tiny sparks can very quickly become massive raging wild fires. We did not want that to happen to us again, and so we built processes into our programme to support that behaviour and promote honest, open and transparent discussion.

This happened in our training base at Bisham Abbey and it happened out in Rio at the Olympic Games. Every morning without fail we walked to and from breakfast together, we would do our individual exercises and activation in the same space, and then we would sit in a circle, as we always did, so we could make eye contact and provide a space to talk. Sometimes it was just a quick catch-up and some admin. Other times there were weightier issues to discuss, and discuss them we did.

One poignant moment for me came when, having decided as a group to come off social media for the duration of the games so that we could focus and be present with each other, the BBC wanted one of the team to write a social media blog. Now in teams gone by this could have been one of those tiny sparks that set players off chatting with their roommate on the way back to their apartment or a shared apartment conversation over a cup of tea that evening. But on this occasion before I, or another member of the leadership group, could address this with the group, another player raised her hand in our morning meeting and brought this issue to our circle. There was understandable resentment from some, jealousy from others and an underlying feeling that our team's decision was being disrespected by pretty much everyone. So, we talked it through: it was heated, it was honest and it was uncomfortable. I have never been prouder of a process in my life. We made a team decision that people could input into it should they wish and that it would be more of a team blog in feel. The final critical step to ensure we did 'stamp out fires early' was that each of us needed to take personal responsibility to not fan the flame after the meeting. Processes allow your behaviours to live in everyone. They have to matter and exist all of the time if you want them to count in the end.

HELEN: Moving on to our 'We are winners' value, part of it was about winning hockey matches, plain and simple. We'd never won anything before, so we had to learn how to win. We needed a process that was going to give an opportunity for all of the behaviours grouped under that value to exist in our training environment. One of those processes became known as 'Thinking Thursday'. We were challenged by our coaches in a variety of ways, but during our Thursday-morning pitch session this was taken to another level.

'Thinking Thursday' embodied the essence of the value 'We are winners'. It was essentially a mini tournament of small-sided games with varying instructions, rules and point-scoring systems. We knew we needed to be ready for anything, and the rules could, and did change, throughout the session, often only being communicated through the assigned 'captains' for that day. Chaos was created, and we had to learn to deal with it in the moment, by ourselves. 'We play smart – we train smart.'

Processes aren't always boring steps that need to be completed in order to get something done; they can be complicated, nuanced, and actually create enthusiasm and motivation. These were hard, competitive sessions, and because of the mental and physical stress we were deliberately being put under, I loved and loathed them in equal measure. It would have been so easy to get waylaid with the strain every week, but the fact I knew this was a process we needed to go through in order to achieve the outcome we wanted kept me level-headed. When you keep your processes, and the reason why you're carrying them out, in mind, they will help you get through challenging moments and situations within your organisational context.

That's how a process taught us how to win.

We also used the 'Thinking Thursday' session to work on penalties under pressure. I've heard football players and managers say there's no point in practising them because it's impossible to recreate the same pressure you'll face in a shootout. It *is* hard to recreate it exactly – they're right on that – but there are many things you can train for that will make a difference, and this session on a Thursday morning did just that. With so much emotion tied up in winning the pressure was immensely high on every single penalty awarded. On top of that they were physically hard sessions, and coming towards the end of the week meant fatigue levels were always high. As I stood over that ball, I would be facing a goalkeeper who knew my strengths and the likely areas I would go to. I had to believe in my ability to beat them, even if they knew where I was going to put the ball. I had to block out all of the unwanted 'noise'. I had to learn to take a deep breath and focus within seconds, even when I was bent over double and gasping for breath.

This session had everything. Winning was the overall desired outcome, and winning requires many things to happen. This process was created to make our value of 'We are winners' come alive. You won't be having to take penalties, I grant you that, but I'm sure you'll face pressure, so put processes in place that help you deliver when you need to. Like us, this might look like practising under pressure, or it might involve providing support mechanisms. What does your team need? Create your processes and make your values live and breathe.

KATE: Helen's right, but you've got to remember that not all processes are created equal! The benefit of having a set of detailed actions in place to support a desired outcome is that they can be trialled, reviewed, and either continued or binned. In 2010 we decided that we needed a strategy to aid our ability to challenge one another in the team. We needed upskilling on the intricacies of giving and receiving honest player to player feedback. As a result of this, we developed a process called 'The Forum'. This method of challenge was applicable to those occasions where a player-to-player conversation just hadn't garnered the desired change in behaviour. Once other avenues to support the player being challenged had been explored, they would be taken to the Forum.

The intention behind the Forum was to bring players who weren't displaying agreed team behaviours in front of the group to be challenged in a supportive way. But it proved to be brutal, and it was immediately clear that this was not the right process for this team. We were a thoughtful nurturing group, and the Forum cut across a great deal of personal values. So, after we tried it with two players, we reviewed it and then duly scrapped it. Reviewing processes allows you to see what strengths you have in your group and what you need from yourself and each other in order to succeed in your ultimate goal. We went back to the player-to-player challenge, and the leadership group was more considered about who was the best person to approach players and provide challenge in a supportive way.

A team that never tries anything new and plays it safe is likely missing out on better ways of working and a chance to examine themselves more deeply. This is a great example of what has been coined 'failing forward' by many, and most notably by John C. Maxwell in his book *Failing Forward: Turning Mistakes into Stepping Stones for Success*. After trying out the Forum once, we realised it was a misstep for this group, and we then used this knowledge to project us forwards to find a better way of utilising challenge within our team.

Critical moments

HELEN: Any form of selection, in any part of life, is challenging. From picking teams in the playground, to selection for an Olympic Games, it is the one constant in sport, and its attack on us as people, especially the ego, is brutal. In the business world, 'selections', such as promotions, can be equally painful, and, as in a sports team, these decisions have the potential to disrupt even the most settled group. When a 'selection' is on the horizon, every sense is heightened. Every look, every comment made, or feedback given is analysed to an inch of its life. Our selections were made relatively close to the tournament itself, so, just when you're needing everything to come together, the tension was thick with anxiety-driven unease.

It's not possible to eradicate that tension altogether. However, there are processes that can be put in place to allow everyone to deal with the situation as best as they can. The first and most important thing to do is to face up to it. It's going to be hard. Let's not pretend it'll be anything else, and the sooner everyone appreciates that the better. So acknowledge it, and name it. Predict how you might feel as an individual. What might happen to your behaviour around that time, and how you might react to others when feeling stressed? Plans can then be made for what you need, both personally and collectively.

Openness, transparency and clear communication will always be crucial around selections. As a group we chose to hear about selection via email. We knew the day and exact time, so we could choose whom to surround ourselves with, if anyone. Selection for Rio was after a week's training and matches in the Netherlands, so 6pm on the Friday night was chosen because that was when the player with the furthest distance to travel from the airport would be home by. We were encouraged to have conversations with some of our closest friends within the team, or teammates we lived with, way in advance of the big day to determine a strategy of support if it was needed or even to have a signal for 'Please leave me alone'!

Think about the timing of any 'selections' you may have. Ours were made at the end of a training block, so players had a natural break away from the group. Although a week doesn't make much difference when you've just had your heart broken, it's better than nothing.

Critical moments are named thus for a reason. If you don't get them right, they have the propensity to set in motion a downward spiral away from your vision. Identifying what your critical moments are is the first step to getting them right. Standing up to them and getting everything out on the table is next. Then make a plan. However hard it is, follow through with the processes you have put in place when your mind wasn't clogged by the pressures or anxieties or any other emotion that that moment might induce.

KATE: There are few tougher moments than selection for an elite athlete. It is vital for individual well-being and group morale to get the supporting processes right for such critical moment. However, another key time in the life of an elite athlete, and in fact any person in a team environment, is the very beginning of the journey. Part of the challenge of joining a team with pre-established visions, values and behaviours is that it can be hard to fully align yourself or have the same sense of ownership as the current team members. On the flip side, it can be challenging for members of the established team to spend time building layers of trust and belief in new members.

Having new people come into a high-pressure competitive environment has the potential to be a hugely positive spring-board moment or the start of a downward spiral. Some of this will depend on the people involved, but in large part the outcome will be down to your culture. Our psychologist, Andrea Furst, brought the concept of a Welcome Ceremony to the leadership group as a way to harness the positivity of the culture and ensure that new players were quickly brought on board and the team continued its forward momentum. At first, I really wasn't sure about the concept. I couldn't connect the meaning with the purpose. I was struggling to ratify how this would help integrate new players and maintain a steady ship. However, the reshaping and/or reformation of a group needs to be managed with honesty and integrity. A Welcome Ceremony gave us a chance to grip the situation and ensure that the outcome was a positive one.

As a group we were once again empowered to build a process/ceremony that reflected our culture and welcomed a new player with clarity and care. A process such as this could tick a lot of boxes for your team. Not only will it inform the new team members about who you are and what they now belong to, it will also serve as a timely reminder of your culture for the whole group or organisation. Regardless of whether the leader changes or the team members change, this is something that could function as long as there is a team. Authentic processes that bring clarity and help you celebrate your culture can be used tactfully across many other areas of your team environment.

HELEN: A sudden change of leadership would count as another critical moment. Take a moment to think about one of the leaders in your life, your manager maybe, your boss, your coach or even your partner, someone you rely on to do their job day to day and lead the way in big moments. Now imagine you're about to take on, as a team, that biggest moment of your career or life, and, for whatever reason, that leader can't be there. Who takes over? Do you know? And would you know what to do?

In the lead-up to the London Olympics no stone was left unturned. We had plans for so many eventualities, some of which we as players were privy to, some we were not. For some we were also included in the discussions, such as what would happen if Kate, as our captain, was to get injured. Unfortunately, Kate was no stranger to getting hit (despite my best coaching advice to 'use your stick!'), so this was a real possibility. Taking everything into consideration, including Kate's and my relationship, and to avoid any doubt, it was decided that I, as vice-captain, would take over as captain in such an eventuality.

With four minutes left of the clock in our first match of the London Olympics, Kate had her jaw broken by the stick of one of our Japanese opponents. This was clearly a horrific injury for Kate personally – as well as the whole team – to have to deal with, but in that moment we had to try to put our emotions to one side, in order to prepare for our next match, which was in less than 48 hours' time. I was obviously upset for Kate, and was processing a lot myself, so one thing I was grateful for was the preparation we'd done. Although our coach had a little wobble, following the processes we had put in place I led the team out for two matches before Kate returned after having had surgery.

Without such pre-set processes it is all too easy to be derailed by an unexpected event or the absence of a crucial person within your team. So, make a plan. It's important to have these discussions well in advance when the air is clear and free of any unusual emotions that could cloud decision making. Yes, you may not need to execute on this plan, and hopefully you won't, but not using it is much better than not having one when you need it.

The penalty shootout

KATE: Emotions and clouded decision making are certainly what spring to mind when I think about penalty shootouts in sport. How often have we been enraptured by the winning save or fateful missed penalty over the years? What we don't tend to think about, though, are the numerous, painstakingly detailed steps that are worked through, long before any penalty is even taken. Well, that's what happens in an ideal world! It seems odd to break down such a powerful sporting moment into a set of process steps, but that is exactly what is required. The way our penalty takers and goalkeepers trained for a penalty shootout that might never happen was methodical, statistically driven and repetitive. When faced with a high-pressure, high-emotion situation we needed to consider a few important factors beforehand to help us thrive in this situation.

HELEN: As one of the penalty takers I'll give a few examples of what this actually meant in practice. Some processes were gone through before the tournament and some during the competition itself. All of it was born out of experience, and, of course, plenty of failure. My biggest lesson was learned during a 2–2 draw against the Netherlands at the Champions Trophy in 2012. I hadn't prepared myself physically or mentally to take a penalty before the game, so when we got one in the game my body shrunk and my mind literally said 'no'. I looked away; I didn't want to take it. Someone else offered, and hesitantly I agreed. They missed, and I wanted the ground to swallow me up. It was decided at half-time that, if we were to get another penalty, then a third person was to take it. We did, and she also missed. Again, I felt sick. After the game I reflected on what had happened. Simply put, the fear of missing had got the better of me. I didn't ever want to let that happen again, so I put a process in place to make sure it didn't. First of all, I would clarify with the coach that he really wanted me to take penalties; any doubt around this really affected me. Before every game I would say to myself that I wanted to take them and where I would put them. When the whistle went, I would actively stand taller, step forwards with conviction, and be happy that we'd won a penalty.

Time made for regular practice was necessary to get into the groove and to reinforce techniques and cues. As often as possible this was done as if we were in a real competition. We made sure we included the long walk from the halfway line because on that long walk you can go from being the most confident player in the world to a nervous wreck in a matter of moments. To skip this part is foolish. Consistently going through the process of the whole routine allowed us to formulate words and phrases to get us to an optimal mindset. Uninvolved teammates would sometimes be asked to shout abuse to put us off. This was about blocking out unwanted noise, even the internal stuff. Interestingly, silence was actually worse, so that when the Dutch fans booed as I made my long walk in the Olympic final, I actually smiled to myself. It made me angry. Anger is good for me, so I channelled it!

How we wanted to feel and be portrayed by the opposition if a shootout was to happen had been discussed and practised to the nth degree. When the whistle went for the end of the game, most of us smiled. Smiling is a good thing to do in most situations to manage stress. It also shows we are confident and in control. The process of deciding on the penalty takers had been decided before the game so we just waited for Danny to come down from the stands to confirm the takers and the order. All five of us gave off positive vibes (regardless of what we were feeling inside), standing tall, head up, chest out. Research has shown that celebrating if you score does wonders for your own team and also deflates the opposition. Interestingly, how you walk back after missing also has an impact, so after I missed my running penalty I knew I had to move confidently back to my team, high-five and get myself prepared for if I got to have another go.

When I was taking my penalty from the spot, all I was thinking was 'tight core', 'tight right hand' and 'push through three balls instead of one'. I knew that, if I did these things, I would put my body in its best state physically, strong and low. I couldn't control what happened after I released the ball or what the goal-keeper did, so I didn't think about that.

KATE: To enable you to have any form of process-driven structure about a known critical moment, you must first take responsibility and ownership of this moment. Organisations must have the courage to make sure time and resources are available to teams wanting to put processes around critical moments. If, for example, you would like to lead a business pitch to a client, but you're not 100 per cent certain because you've not done the work or got yourself in the optimal place to do the pitch, you will hesitate and so will those around you. Through practice and perseverance in the processes, you will learn that you can deliver excellence consistently.

To carry this business pitch analogy forward to the practice part of the penalty-taking process, you are going to have to go the whole hog! If you think you can just turn up and turn it on when you need to, you might be right on the odd occasion, but in order to achieve consistent levels of excellence it's going to require some thorough and honest preparation. Even going into the detail of practising walking into and out of the room can make the difference. Knowing the layout of the room, the tech set-up, the seating arrangement and so on will help you visualise in colour. When you follow this process through from start to finish, ensuring that there is ample space for last-minute hiccups and alterations, you will really flourish and perform at your best.

It's important to consider how we frame these critical moment situations in our minds. Breaking the moment down into smaller manageable parts also allows your brain to really focus on the execution of the detail towards the desired outcome. If you find yourself staring at a pitch briefing document and feeling the intense pressure of it weighing you down, just press pause for a few minutes. Give yourself some space to breathe and think about how you can break the pitch into its simplest form. What do they want/need? What can we bring/deliver? How will we go about that?

And remember, athletes train for years for one single moment in time. So, practise and form the habits you want to rely on under pressure. Practise in different environments and with lots of varied obstacles or problems to contend with. Train hard and play easy. By mentally, physically and emotionally preparing yourself, you can actually come to enjoy the very same high-pressure moment that perhaps now you fear the most.

Value your people

KATE: It might be assumed that processes have a very serious focus and are all about aligning behaviour and navigating critical moments. In some ways perhaps they are, but processes can also help celebrate success and award achievement. We often forgot, while on a quest for excellence, to really enjoy the moments of accomplishment along the way. In fact, enjoying these moments together as a team can have a significant bonding effect. When individual achievements are recognised and acknowledged we feel valued as team members, and when we feel valued, we give more to the team. All of this leads to greater team performance and a happy high-functioning team.

In our centralised programme we were able to really take hold of this process in a number of formal and informal ways. Birthdays were a great opportunity to have a big lunch together or cut cake together. Although we were spending a lot of time in each other's company, this was more often than not in training sessions or meetings. If people could make it, going into the local village for a casual lunch gave us time to relax and chat about life, a TV box set, anything! Such moments are subtle subconscious team-building exercises and, some might argue, far more fun than an awayday spent on an assault course!

As players we also wanted to put processes in place where we could formally celebrate player milestones or achievements reached in our international careers. How we acknowledged a player's first, one hundredth or very last international cap mattered. Again, it comes back to how you are valued as a person in that organisation or team. When we feel valued, we also feel respected. We helped push the governing body to acknowledge players when they retired, to thank them for their service. The foundation for all of these celebratory moments taking place is good processes. If you know who is to be acknowledged, at what point and by whom, anybody can take the lead and make it happen. Unfortunately for us there weren't always concrete processes in place, and so some people slipped through the net and were not celebrated as they should have been. When you don't value your people equally, you are creating undercurrents that are likely to have a huge impact at some point down the line.

Celebrating the small moments can easily be glossed over as a 'nice to have'. But consider how you would feel being singled out for praise from your boss or your colleagues in front of your team? Of course, some people could not think of anything worse! But the majority of us would on some level take great pride in that moment. Even a card passed around with small comments from your teammates about your achievement will have a telling effect on you and, significantly, the team. For birthdays or major milestones, we would send a card around the team, particularly if we were away on tour, and everyone would write a little personal note inside. I've kept all of mine, and they are some of my most treasured possessions. In this small way you show you care and that you're invested in one another's achievements. These things make you more of a team and less of a group. Processes such as this make us feel valued and give us a sense of belonging.

Processes can be powerful cultural tools, supporting team habits and show-casing team behaviours. At their best, they keep the team moving forward, towards the collective vision. At their worst, they fail, yet even the failure of a process can lead to positive future action. When utilised strategically, processes are an effective way to make culture a day-to-day habit. They are a way to weave the team's vision, values and behaviours into everything your team does.

When teams have systematic steps to follow, via their processes, team members can focus on delivering their individual role with absolute clarity. This enables people to feel valued and understand their worth to the team.

The conversations a team shares to form critical moment processes, such as selection, help build empathy and psychological safety. Following through on processes and reviewing them diligently also builds trust and respect among the group. All of these factors are absolutely essential to any consistently high-performing team.

Building processes into your working day helps raise the awareness levels of team members and of the team as a whole. Great teams have great self-awareness, which in turn fosters a deep interconnectivity. When we are connected as a team we move in synergy. Team processes are a tangible way to create this alignment within the group. This all needs to be led from the top and from within.

Leadership is vital to every aspect of team culture that we have touched on so far in this book, none more so than processes. In the following chapter we will explore the importance of great leadership: what it takes to lead and what the markers of good leadership are.

Team huddle

Talking about and formulating your team processes can seem a little dry and boring. So, it's important that you make this as creative and as interactive as possible. Use the different points of view in your team as your greatest strength as you find new ways to be super-efficient, high-functioning and collectively oriented towards your vision.

Questions to consider

- How can you break your team values down into strategic or behavioural steps?
- When are people at capacity in your team with stress, workload or pressure?
- When you are at your most stretched as a team, are you able to function optimally. What does that look, sound and feel like?
- Does everyone feel valued in your team?
- How do you celebrate successes and milestones in your team?

Key team tactics

- Begin exploring the most basic processes in your team and follow the chain of work from start to finish. Notice where the lines of communication are and the quality of those linkages. Are there any inefficiencies or blockages in the system as it stands? Be thorough and creative with your reviewing.
- Sometimes processes are so common you don't even realise you are working within them every day! It's a good idea to draw or illustrate your processes in some way to look at them with fresh eyes. How many steps are there currently? Can any be removed? Do any steps

need adding? Working collaboratively here will really benefit team understanding.

- Document what you learn about your processes. What is important and why? Where is their room for improvement and why? As situations, people and environments change, so too may your processes. Doing the work as you go along will help you stay agile in today's modern working world.

- Include all team members in the building of new processes where possible or, at the very least, communicate them with openness and transparency. When we understand why a process is in place, we are far more likely to engage fully with it.

- When assessing your processes, it is always good to start with the question 'Can this be better?' Keep asking that question often of yourself and your teammates and you will not go far wrong.

5

Leadership

So far in this book we have addressed some of the major foundational aspects we believe every consistent high-performing team needs to support great culture. Although this chapter is titled 'Leadership', it's not, of course, the only relevant chapter for leaders – the whole book in its essence is about leadership. We also think it's important to state that leadership is also not just about 'assigned' leaders; we believe we can all lead, and therefore, whoever you are and whatever your role, this chapter is for you!

Dictionary definitions of leadership are centred around guidance and direction towards a common goal. How we define our leaders and what we consider to be successful leadership is ever evolving. As more research is done on the impact of leaders, new trends are made and followed and old ones are discarded and discredited. When we look back to the styles of leadership we grew up with versus what is the trend today, it is like night and day. In any case, regardless of the definition or style, one thing is eternally true: for better or worse, every leader leaves a trace.

We are all influenced heavily by those who lead us, particularly in our formative years, and throughout our lives. Through our interactions with leaders, we learn to lead ourselves. In the most successful periods of the GB women's hockey team, every team member was considered a leader and we were, at the same time, all being led – from above the team and from within the team. In this chapter we will look in detail at how this delicate leadership balancing act was conceptualised and navigated.

Leadership is a never-ending quest, a constant search for better. For some people this concept might seem daunting, like swimming upstream against a tidal wave of theories and methodologies. It is daunting, and it is hard work. But it is important for ourselves and the people whom we lead that we know we can and we will do this hard work. In this chapter *we will be candid in sharing our experiences of leadership. We will look at how great teams are led, how leadership has evolved, and how it can be developed in people and teams. In detailing our learnings from both leading and being led, we will highlight some key themes and concepts that we believe are critical to help you thrive as a leader.*

Lead from within

KATE: For centuries the command-and-control style of leadership was the way to get things done and to get people to do things for you. Any deviation away from this status quo was considered a bit 'hippy' or 'fluffy'. In very broad general terms, white, middle-class men led in an autocratic manner, and the rest of us followed or copied them in order to get ahead. This was how it was done and, in many areas of life, is still being done. I grew up thinking leadership was about having a loud voice, commanding the troops and being hyper-dictatorial, and, since I was relatively shy as a young person, leadership for me seemed an unrealistic and terrifying prospect. It didn't help that many of the leaders I was surrounded by led in exactly this way.

What we think, we become. Because I thought leadership was about being something that I wasn't, I tried to become a certain type of leader. I didn't lead from within, I led from the outside in. At the beginning of my captaincy, I attempted to lead like those that had gone before me – in particular a woman named Sue Chandler who I felt was a phenomenal leader. Sue always seemed to have the right words to say in any given moment and connected with everyone she led. I took to making inspirational points in team huddles and big speeches before games. One such opportunity presented itself before the final of the KT Cup in South Korea in 2003. I wrote an 'epic' speech that likened the contest to the South Korean flag. I referenced the yin and yang symbol that sits in the centre of the flag and detailed how we needed balance in our side to win the game. I went on to detail how the four symbols represented in the corners of the flag would need to be brought to life in order to overcome our opponents. What I hadn't noticed was that it hadn't stopped raining for the entirety of our rest day and the pitch was water-logged, making the game unplayable. The speech went into the bin, where it belonged! I took this as a message from on high, but perhaps it came from within. Being captain wasn't about trying to be like Sue, or indeed anyone else, but myself. Sue was such an amazing leader because she was authentic and utterly at peace with herself. I didn't know what type of leader I was, or who I was, and that is where my work began.

Not only were my big oratorical moments a complete waste of time for me, they were not having any impact on the players I was leading. I needed to take time to reflect and be curious about myself. What are my values? What principles do I truly stand by? What strengths do I have and how could I build on those? These are the questions we must all ask ourselves if we want to develop as leaders and as people.

For much of my early captaincy I had imposter syndrome on a grand scale, and this had a deep impact on my connection with players and the relationships we formed. I believe people were willing to follow me, even from the beginning of my captaincy, because I led by example scrupulously. However, I wasn't getting the best of myself or others because I wasn't taking the time to get to know myself and others in an authentic way. I spent the rest of my captaincy from 2003 onwards trying to learn this lesson, among others. My ability to be open with myself and others would help me be the best of me and help my teammates be the best of them. The more I spoke from the heart and lived wholeheartedly, the more players were prepared to follow me and do the same. It was only then that we as individuals and as a collective really began to thrive. This didn't happen overnight, and I am still wrangling with it today.

Thankfully, there is an ever-increasing depth of new research and with it new understanding about effective leadership. That, together with increased access to psychologists and to popular books, documentaries and podcasts on the topic, means that our leadership horizons are being continually broadened. This breadth and depth of information will support your ability to be open to finding a more effective way to lead. Inevitably, it is going to take a fair bit of soul searching and a need to reflect on your values, principles and strengths as a leader. Having the mentality that you can always do it better is a good trait to lean on when it comes to leadership. That ability to have a curious mind and a desire to be authentic are excellent leadership attributes you can foster and value.

HELEN: Taking time to figure out who you are and consider what kind of a leader you want to be is the first step. But there is also a very important ethical perspective to consider. Some years ago now, we had a coach who instructed his manager to take one of our teammate's stick bags to the bottom of the drive at Lilleshall National Sports Centre while we were warming up for our session. The drive at Lilleshall is about two miles long, and when we'd finished the warm-up the coach coolly told our teammate where her stick bag was, and that she had to run to the end of the drive to collect it before she could join in with the session. We were all a bit confused, to be honest. We even gathered together spare shin-pads and a stick for her to borrow, thinking it might be some kind of team resilience test. The coach hadn't been in the job long, and a hopeful part of us wondered whether it was some kind of weird joke, and all would be resolved with laughs and smiles – a funny story we'd be able to reminisce over for years to come. Sadly, we were miles off. When she returned and joined us on the pitch around 30 minutes later, he just tore into her. In front of everyone he wielded his power over her, and us all, and ripped her apart.

To this day Kate and I don't get it. The only thing that seems clear to us is that he wanted to let her know, and probably all of us know, that he was in charge. This was his way of doing things, which certainly became apparent over time, and in actual fact he made no apologies for it. You could say he was being authentic. That's who he was, that's how he'd decided he wanted to be as a coach and leader, and so that's what he did. This leads on to a very important caveat to leading from your authentic self: it has to get the best out of your people.

This leader was using his desire to be 'in charge' as an excuse to lead the way he did. Other leaders may feel that a perceived inability to communicate is an excuse to lead in a siloed and isolated way. It is easy for all of us to retreat into 'the way we are' and use this as an excuse or reason for why we behave the way we do. But we are not static beings. We can flex and mould our authentic style to different people and different situations without compromising our values and principles. If you lead from within and with the individuals you lead in mind, you will build much stronger connections, create better performances, and foster a greater sense of fulfilment for you and your people.

Getting the best out of your people

HELEN: Society has long put leaders up on a pedestal and look to those leaders to display some very specific traits. We have then hired or voted in leaders who fit this narrow mould, and for a time we have got stuck in this cyclic rhythm. How to be an effective leader, though, is changing. With more emphasis being placed on well-being and personal development, being of service is beginning to take precedence over being served. Now, more than ever, recruiting leaders based on their ability to create an environment where their team can thrive is critical. Nonetheless, many people continue to find themselves thrust into leadership positions because they are good at the technical aspects of their job and despite their never having given any support to developing people. The next three subsections highlight some of the most important factors we believe can help any leader get the best from the people they lead.

Building relationships

HELEN: How does it make you feel when you're greeted with eye contact every morning alongside a simple 'hello' from your boss? And the flip side: what's the difference when you're barely acknowledged as you make your way to your desk?

We probably all know someone who doesn't say 'Good morning' as they walk through the door. We may even be that person. I hate to admit it, but it's definitely been me from time to time. I would sometimes get bogged down in the daily grind and my own personal struggle, and it felt as though engaging with the outside world would just cost me too much. Over time I realised that making the effort to hold my head up and to look people in the eye was actually the best medicine for my own weary body and mind. Connecting with the people around me was the light I needed to thrive. It's the same for us all. We all need to feel seen. To feel valued and listened to. As a leader, the connections and relationships you build with your team are so fundamental in getting the best out of them. And it really can start with a 'hello'.

I think back to another coach we had. I was injured for a lot of the time that she was in post, it was when I was struggling with my ankle injury which left me side-lined for two years. She was a very different coach from the one I described above, and that became abundantly clear when one day, out of the blue, a card dropped through my letterbox. It was from her. I couldn't possibly tell you what it said, but the fact that I can remember that she sent it tells you how it made me feel. I had been out of the squad for some time, I wasn't much use to her, and yet here she was, taking time to think about how I might be feeling at that moment. One of the most common complaints I heard from fellow hockey players and athletes from other sports was how they were made to feel worthless when they were injured. At a time when you're struggling the most, when you need more help than ever before, it was like we were invisible.

For me, empathy has grown to be one of the most valuable traits a leader can possess. It might have been somewhere on my list ten years ago, but it wouldn't have even registered when I first got into the squad twenty-odd years ago. If you're able to put yourself in someone else's shoes, especially as a leader, you have the chance to make a connection that builds relationships based on trust and respect. There is nothing more powerful than your actions saying, 'I get it, and I care.'

As a leader, this was definitely not something that came naturally to me. I now find myself being weirdly grateful for some of my harder life experiences, like my parents getting divorced, my injuries, losing matches and tournaments, the social pressures of being in a same-sex relationship and my mental health struggles. The feelings that came with each and every one of them taught me that life is hard. You never know what someone might be going through. We all have a story that has got us to where we are today, and that perspective shapes our views and opinions, our behaviours and our moods. There is nothing more worthwhile than trying to understand who your people are underneath their work persona, and giving them permission to be their full selves, whatever that is. This is not easy work. Most of us struggle to understand ourselves, let alone anyone else. Building relationships takes time and a lot of effort, and coming from a place of genuine care gives this process the best chance of succeeding.

KATE: It is often the smallest gestures that have the greatest impact. One club coach gave us all a small slip of paper before the playoff final at the end of the season, and on it were what he felt our strengths were and what our value to the team was. This piece of paper got a bit grotty because I kept it in my gumshield box for a very long time! I either looked at it specifically or was at least reminded of it every time I put my gumshield in; this would have been pretty much daily and sometimes two or three times a day. That bit of care to write that personal note to me reminded me of who I was and what I was excellent at. It boosted my confidence and made me feel strong and powerful. All from one tiny bit of paper and a whole lot of care from one coach being prepared to tell me what he valued in me. He was seeing me for who I was and actually demanding it from me in some ways. He did this for the whole team, and so the impact was magnified and amplified. We won the playoff final, but more importantly than that he won our respect and trust.

As we have highlighted previously in this chapter, leadership has evolved in both theory and delivery style. The importance of forging strong relationships between leaders and those being led is now much better understood and widely accepted. In a sporting environment coaches are aiming to unlock the potential of athletes in their care. In a business environment the desire should be the same. In either case I believe the best way of achieving this is by actively developing relational coaching. Relational coaching – which is hardly new as a concept – places the coach–player relationship at the centre of the process, with the weight placed on the perspective of the person being coached. I would wager that the best experiences you've had of being coached or led is when you have trusted that the coach or leader has your best interests at heart, that they are invested in your ambitions and you as a person, when you are working together towards a common goal and you are both committed to inputting energy into your joint journey. Whatever the context, be it business or sport, a leader's ability to communicate with openness and clarity will fuel the interpersonal relationship and move development towards a mutually successful outcome. One small slip of paper can go a long way!

Empowering people

KATE: Building relationships between leaders and followers is multi-layered and multifaceted. Leaders can build trust in many ways, and empowering the people you lead is one of the best ways to do this. It is also one of the most challenging things you can do as a leader, depending on who you are and what your instinctive style of leadership is. There must be an acceptance as an empowering leader that things can go wrong and mistakes may be made by those you've empowered. You may even feel that you could have prevented the error or mistake if you had executed the task yourself. But if you are able to empower your people through the successes and failures and embrace the risk, the payoff will be huge. The development and growth of your people will be more than worth any perceived risk. If you are also able to share the fact that this process is difficult, it helps build trust, because as a leader you are inevitably making yourself vulnerable. On presenting the idea of a centralised programme for the very first time, our coach, Danny Kerry, effectively asked the group if they wanted to join him on this journey. He could have just said: 'This is what I think is best. Get on board or leave.' Instead, he chose to open the decision making on the direction of travel to the group.

In that one meeting, Danny opened himself up to the group in a way he hadn't done before. It was a really important moment in lots of ways and the start of something very special. From that moment onwards, Danny was more prepared to devolve leadership. I'm sure it wasn't easy for him, and although he didn't do it all the time, when he did, the team as a whole inevitably reaped the rewards.

Another great example of how Danny's empowering leadership style benefited the group was when he included the players in building the process around how selections were announced. As we've seen in Chapter 4, selection is effectively about breaking hearts and making dreams come true. This process is brutal for an athlete and is like an abiding dark cloud hanging over everybody's head. Nobody can soften the blow of a non-selection, but what management can do is be respectful of players and understanding of the process. By including the people you lead in the formulation of such high-stakes processes, you give some element of control back at a time when control seems very much out of their hands. By asking and encouraging them to discuss it as a group in minute detail – when, how and by whom – you respect the importance of the moment for them. Empowerment builds empathy and solidifies a shared understanding, all of which are fundamental to trust.

My last example of empowering leadership is possibly the most challenging of all for a leader: giving up control to the team to vote for the team's leadership group. To say to the team, 'Now it is you who are leading; I trust you to select the leaders from within your group,' is fairly bold. People are often quite taken aback when we tell them that this is how we came to be assigned as leaders in the team. I can imagine how daunting for a head coach or team leader it must be to devolve these important decisions when you are perhaps not fully assured what the resulting vote will reveal and what direction the leadership group will take the team. It helped that we voted for our leadership group *after* we had established our culture and we knew we were voting for people who would lead us on that cultural journey. As a leader, if you have established a clear mandate and know the group well enough to know the competence levels, then it is a bold but brave move to back their choices. The trust between the players and leadership group was strong because they knew they had voted to be led by these players. The relationship and trust between the leadership group and the management team was perhaps harder earned because the former hadn't had a vote or a say. However, I believe this is a much better way around than the alternative option of being handed something you don't want or need from on high. Empower your people to take big decisions when there is clarity of purpose and experiential competence and you will see the benefits for yourself. Be brave and be bold.

Safe spaces

HELEN: As Kate described, empowerment involves risk. It's there on both sides: whether you're giving it or receiving it, there needs to be trust and people need to feel safe. The role of the leader in creating spaces that are safe at work is fundamental. You've probably heard of the term 'psychological safety'. It's become a bit of a trendy buzzword over the last decade, and Google made sure of that when it commissioned its own research and discovered that, for teams to be high-performing, *who* is in a team matters much less than *how* it interacts, and psychological safety was identified as the key to positive interaction above anything else. According to Amy Edmondson, a Harvard Business School professor and leading psychological safety expert, this is because within psychologically safe environments there is a belief that team members can voice their views and opinions and, importantly, make mistakes, confident in the knowledge that it will not lead to negative consequences of any kind.

Unfortunately, when theories are talked about in general terms, to some they lose their appeal, or, worse, they're not understood properly. There is a misconception that psychologically safe environments are all about being comfortable and nice to one other all of the time – but in fact this isn't about cosy collaboration, far from it. In order to learn and grow collectively, psychologically safe teams demand and expect challenge; they embrace discomfort and hard conversations because these come from a place of care and support. It's actually about feeling safe enough to feel uncomfortable. You want and need feedback to be better. You want and need your team to speak up, to give their opinions, especially when they are different from your own. How you go about doing this is key, and there are many practical solutions to ensure this happens.

There are both formal and informal hierarchies in most teams. These aren't bad in themselves, but recognising and acknowledging where the power imbalances sit is a good place to start. Leaders need to take the lead in bridging this gap, and being proactive when it comes to communication is crucial. Many of our coaches used to say, 'My door is always open.' I'm sure you've heard it. It's supposed to signify that 'Challenge is welcome, I'm open to it, come and speak to me.' But in fact, the idea behind it is incredibly unfair, because the reality is that it places complete responsibility at everybody else's door rather than their own. Who is doing the walking and knocking, after all? When you really think about it, when you put yourself in the shoes of your newest member and explore the physical and metaphorical journey they'd need to make to knock on their boss's door, how many of them would take them at their word?

Communication is something you do, and leaders have to make it happen. Everyday conversations go a long way in creating safe spaces. I know that when coaches and team leaders showed their human side by expressing emotion or vulnerabilities, by sharing interests or talking about family, it helped to break down the power divide: we realised that they were just like us. It created understanding and strengthened relationships – a hugely valuable commodity when the pressure is on. Being consistent in those pressure moments solidifies that safety even further. Providing opportunity by 'formalising' communication by some degree allows team members to prepare to give feedback or make suggestions. The variety of meetings we had (discussed in Chapter 4) between the player group and staff groups, the 'buddy' groups and the leadership group, all contributed to providing that opportunity. Everyone knew this was a time when the leaders would be ready to listen and be open to hear what was being said without judgement or retribution.

If you're unsure as to how to go about this with your team, ask them! Your people are your biggest resource, and the knowledge that surrounds you is precious. Have the courage to step out of your comfort zone to find out what they're feeling and what would work for them. That's how we settled on having buddy groups. It was a suggestion that came from the team, as not everyone felt comfortable speaking up in the larger group. We had to ensure the whole range of diverse thought from the squad was encapsulated, and the smaller working groups were a great solution. Taking action on a point raised like this also showed that we were listening, greatly increasing the chance of more team members sharing their thoughts. As a leader, your reaction is always vital: be thankful and grateful that someone has taken a risk and spoken up for the good of the team.

Lead yourself, then each other

HELEN: As a leader, you have to take the lead on what you want to see from your team, which ideally will align with your vision, values and behaviours (VVB). You'll have to be one very lucky leader to have a team full of people who are prepared to do what you are not. This sounds obvious, but if all leaders were doing this, leading by example wouldn't be such a special trait for a leader to have. Kate did this very well, in every aspect, although I'm not sure she saw it as such a special leadership trait. That ability to check and challenge yourself first takes a great deal of self-awareness of the impact you will have on your team, not to mention hard work. You will gain respect when you lead by example and put yourself in the best place to challenge others to do the same, and importantly inspire a critical mass to join you. Having that wider group, all living by the agreed culture and taking the lead, will be the difference.

'Do you realise the influence you have on this team?' This question was put to me by our coach during one of my quarterly reviews, and it really did make a difference to my thinking. Before then I knew I made an impact in many different ways, but until it was said to me out loud I hadn't given it as much thought as perhaps I needed to. How I drove the standards in training was one of my strengths, so in general it was a positive point being made to me, but of course there were times when I wasn't feeling it, and instead of just having an off day, I had the potential to drag the team in the wrong direction. My awareness of both of these aspects was equally important, and I needed to be completely honest with myself if I was going to have the impact we needed.

Whether you're an assigned leader or not, take some time to think about the influence you're having on those around you. Ask yourself: are my behaviours representing our values, and am I steering my team closer to our vision or farther away? As a team, we were most successful when everyone understood the impact they were having on each other. Built into the fabric of our culture was a recognition that we all played a role, and that also included the leadership of that culture. First you lead yourself, then you lead each other.

KATE: To underline the point made at the beginning of this chapter, we are all leaders and we all leave a trace. We are having an impact on people whether we believe it or not. The people we lead are feeding off our energy; in fact, all people in our sphere whether we are leading them or not are affected by what we put out into the ether. Energy, both positive and negative, is contagious. *Big red flashing beacon* – this doesn't mean we must all put on masks and pretend everything is good and well when it's not. This is neither authentic nor genuine, and while it may work for you in the short term, in the long run this is going to cost you energy and your mental health.

What I think is important is that we at least acknowledge that we have fluctuating energy levels and that this will have an impact on the people around us. Once we have got comfortable with this fact, then we can start to consider and be curious about how we want to manage this complex situation. I know that I am an emotional person, and that, if I turn up to coach a hockey session having not checked in with my energy beforehand, things are likely to go array. So the walk from the car to the pitch is a little bit of check-in time where I ask myself where I'm at and where I need to be to lead a training session. This is a work in progress: some days I am way off mark, some days I forget to do it at all. Once I've taken my temperature, though, I can implement some small behaviours which help me get to where I need to be. If I'm low mood and low energy, I will want to retreat and become introverted. What I need to be is connected and present. So I try to say 'hello' and make eye contact – two small gestures which have a positive impact on the players I coach and on me as well.

Assessing your energy levels and managing your state is good practice for everybody and the skills we learned through the exercises we've described in Chapter 7 certainly helped with this. The ability to know where you're at as a leader and be able to make changes if necessary requires self-awareness. When our leaders are self-aware, they show authenticity and those are the leaders that we want to follow. If you can get a critical mass to follow you, then you can really bring about cultural change on a grand scale. The term 'critical mass' came into modern consciousness around the year 2000 when Malcolm Gladwell referenced the term in his critically acclaimed book *The Tipping Point: How Little Things Can Make a Big Difference*. It is said that the result of something succeeding or failing is in large part down to whether a certain point of saturation or take-up is reached.

I've been in teams where the critical mass led the team positively towards the collective vision with great success. I have also been in teams that had a critical mass leading against the team culture, resulting in woeful performances and devastating team failure. Critical mass energy is contagious energy which is spread by just a handful of your people. Knowing who holds this transformational power and their potential impact on the group could be a game changer for you and the teams you circulate in. I'm not sure I fully respected just how incredible the leadership within the London 2012 training squad was. There was a critical mass of assigned and non-assigned leaders who used their position as positive cultural influencers in the group. The behavioural and attitudinal progress that was made from 2009 to 2012 was phenomenal. Building on the empowerment we received from Danny as head coach, players took responsibility and drove it from within.

These types of people have very particular and very special social gifts which drive the success of any social trend. We had had teammates with these skillsets before 2009, of course. The difference was that, in the lead-up to the London Olympics, we were given the framework, trust and power to go forth and lead on our culture. These women often required no words, just a unique undefinable trait to lead and have people follow. We were blessed with many people who possessed many of these traits, and it showed in our culture and in our outcomes. I only fully realised the power of this when we lost a lot of those people after London 2012, through retirement and injury, and as, over a two-year period, the atmosphere in the team changed. We lost a lot of players who played a vital role in connecting the smaller friendship groups. With a change of leadership we also lost the voices of the knowledgeable information specialists who could communicate with clarity as we sought to solve problems. And, most vitally, the players who had subtly cajoled and persuaded teammates to live and breathe the culture were replaced by others with more strident voices who sold a new, brasher brand of behavioural and attitudinal norms, and this, in my opinion, played a significant role in the erosion of our once-flourishing team culture. Being conscious of your impact and the energy you bring can be the difference – this is in your gift.

We all have the ability to lead, and we are doing so every day whether we like it or not. We have an impact on our own and other people's lives, and to some extent we get to choose whether that impact is positive or negative. Leadership is about motivating a group of people towards a common goal, and, by putting your people at the centre, you can achieve that in your way and in your style. We are complex multi-layered beings and can draw various parts of our personality out to lead in the appropriate way in specific moments and with specific people. As soon as you free yourself up by removing the obstructions that have been telling you to lead in a specific way, you can start to lead in your own way – and your way is always best for everyone.

We are also not static entities; we have the ability to flex, mould and grow throughout our lives. How you lead now probably wasn't how you led ten years ago. We are surrounded by a wealth of knowledge, research and opinion which can be absorbed in any manner of ways that suit you and your way of operating. Always remember that your greatest resource is the people you lead day to day. Building strong relationships through open and honest interactions in psychologically safe environments will build strong bonds of trust and respect. In the next chapter, we will help you explore the power of embracing vulnerability and how it can ultimately have an impact on you winning together.

Team huddle

You are not born a leader. Leaders are made through hard work and continual growth. A deep knowledge and understanding of yourself and those around you can help you lead from a place of authenticity and vulnerability. These are the brave leaders we grow to trust, respect and follow.

Questions to consider

- What are your values and how do you want to lead?
- Are you getting the best from your team?
- Where are you emotionally now and where do you need to be?
- Do you regularly ask for feedback from your whole team?
- How do you connect with your people on a daily, weekly and monthly basis?
- As a leader do you trust that there is an understanding of intent, required competency and clarity of role in your team?
- Where do you go to update, refresh and get challenged on your thoughts on leadership?

Key team tactics

- To gauge where your energy levels are, you can practise a few different visualization techniques and see what works for you. It could be an image of yourself, an object that relates to how you feel, a colour ... or simply a score out of ten. Try a few of these techniques and see what helps. Remember, just the process of checking in with your energy levels this way will help you be mindful and present.
- Ask for some feedback from the people you lead. It can be anonymous responses, a chat over a brew or a walk

with a colleague – whatever you feel comfortable with and feels right for you and your team. Ask a few questions and listen. *Really* listen. Take it all in and absorb it for the gift that it is. Feel all the emotions you need to feel, and think about why you are feeling the way you do. Then make sure you follow up with words and actions.

- Consider where you can devolve control to your team. It's a good exercise to think through what the clarity of purpose and procedure would be if you weren't present as a leader. If you're unsure, it might help to work through the questions above. If you believe they can fly, then set them free!

- Consider the power of small gestures: checking in, making eye contact, saying hello. Don't be afraid to make mistakes, grow with them and take your team with you on this journey. Find something that is authentic to you and your team.

- Write down the name of each member of your team and what it is you really value in them. Consider what is their speciality and why that is so important to the team. Just doing this process alone will be enlightening for you, and if you can find the courage to share your thoughts with them, it has the potential to be game changing for you all.

- If you feel like you might be stuck in the mud as a leader, reach out to your network and ask them what they've read, listened to, watched recently that's prompted them to think about leadership. We are not static entities: you can find motivation and inspiration for change everywhere – in books, documentaries, podcasts, TED Talks, to name but a few.

6

Vulnerability

Many people commented that we really looked like a team after our final performance in Rio. They were probably reacting to, and commenting on, our physical closeness and our connected interactions both on and off the field of play. They saw a tight-knit group, all together, having one another's backs and a single collective purpose. We certainly believe that some of that external 'look' can be attributed to these points. In our opinion, how we made these spectators feel on that balmy evening was in fact largely down to the things they could not see – our many moments of vulnerability that we shared, owned and grew connections from.

How did we go about opening up to ourselves and to one another? What is vulnerability and what did that look like in reality? In this chapter we will delve into our own personal journey of vulnerability as well as that of the team to explain how we became so strongly connected. We will lay out the processes that did and didn't work for us, and why. We will establish that, for a team to function at its optimum level and for individuals within that team to thrive, vulnerability, connection and trust must be present and nurtured. We will also show you how a team can quickly slip into being dysfunctional when none of this is in place.

Vulnerability is not a comfortable place for most people. For us, certainly, it was hard work. None of us found it easy, and to this day both of us continue to wrangle with it on a daily basis. But this is where the magic lives. This chapter, more than any other, will show you how to go from good to great. You can have an inspiring vision, values and even behaviours, but, unless you are prepared to do this work from a place of vulnerability, both as individuals and as a team, you will never fully realise your collective potential. Through vulnerability we found courage, joy, love, belonging, trust and truth. Let's get comfortable with our discomfort and begin the journey to living wholeheartedly.

Going 'all in'

HELEN: Such is the importance of vulnerability, we could have easily started with this chapter, for what we did as sportswomen was inherently vulnerable. According to the American research professor and author Brené Brown, vulnerability is defined by 'uncertainty, risk and emotional exposure', and those facets really did consume most of what we did. Every day we were in situations where vulnerability was necessary to achieve the best outcome. Vulnerability is the normal state for all of us: it could be a conversation with the boss, speaking up in a meeting, disagreeing with a colleague, stepping up to lead a project. How vulnerability shows up for each and every one of us in these contexts will differ greatly, and only you will know the situations when you feel most at risk and emotionally exposed. It's in those moments when you have a choice. Do you give yourself to that vulnerability or do your defence mechanisms go up? Do you expose yourself emotionally, or do you play it safe?

Every time we stepped onto the pitch, whether that was for a match or training, we put our whole selves out there to be judged, both externally and internally – both by coaches, teammates, spectators, the press and anyone else ('Are they good enough?') and by ourselves ('Am I good enough?'). Every single time I asked for the ball from a teammate, I was making myself vulnerable. To play it safe would be to hide, to not want the ball at all. But out on that pitch there was no choice. We had to show up. And if you think about it, the same can be said for all aspects of creating an amazing team off the pitch as well, as individuals and as a collective unit. When we chose to set our vision as 'GOLD' for the 2012 Olympic Games, there was absolutely no certainty that we would achieve that. At the time, just uttering the word 'gold' in a vision meeting felt like taking a risk. What if no one agrees? What if I look stupid? What if we actually go for it and we fail? We could have hidden, we could have avoided wanting the ball in that moment because we didn't want to feel uncomfortable. Thankfully, we had the courage to share our innermost doubts and dreams with our teammates, and we were able to achieve something which, maybe at the time, some of the team believed was out of our reach.

KATE: As emotionally revealing as my playing career was, I have found the few years post my retirement from hockey hugely exposing. I have gone from a feeling of knowing to unknowing. Working as a keynote speaker employed to tell my and our story is necessarily exposing. I joke with a great deal of seriousness that it's like therapy every time I take the stage – very public therapy with strangers. And there is certainly a sense of being bare. When Helen and I speak we speak from the heart, and the care we had for the team and our culture is heartfelt and real. My voice breaks regularly when I'm recalling memories or moments, and there have been times when I've completely broken down in tears and grateful that I have Helen by my side.

Writing this book makes me feel hugely vulnerable. Putting our opinions, our thoughts, our failures out there to be scrutinised and analysed feels hard. It feels hard because it is hard, and it is hard because it is sacred. Our personal vulnerabilities are our gift. The safe option, of course, would be to not write this book at all and not share ourselves so personally in keynote speeches. But then those who know us know that we don't take the easy comfortable option very often! The truly great experiences and opportunities for growth lie in those hard-to-reach places ... when we choose to go 'all in'.

All of us are inherently vulnerable when we go 'all in' on something. It could be a new relationship or a new job. None of us can predict the future, and we can't ever say for certain how things will go. There is a real chance that you will fail, and you may very well have failed many times before and yet here you are again showing up fully. That is vulnerability in its rawest form. Making the choice to fully immerse ourselves in the team, our programme and the pursuit of our vision made us exceptionally vulnerable. The same goes for every player in the squad. None of us knew whether we would be selected; every time we stepped onto the pitch to be analysed and assessed we were opening ourselves up fully to every possible outcome. I think that's bravery, and I believe it is this courage that I loved most about my teammates.

There may well be a number of you wondering why we're talking about vulnerability. Isn't success, in sport and life, about strength and power? Isn't vulnerability a weakness to be avoided? There are times when displays of such physical and mental attributes are useful, certainly. On the field of play showing your fragility to the opposition can prove costly. However, to truly have strength is to really be yourself, to accept all of yourself. It is to acknowledge that you are going to feel uncomfortable walking into that meeting and still opening the door. It is to apply for that job when you haven't got an interview on the last 15 attempts. When you show up and share all of yourself, go 'all in', you show strength. What's more, your living courageously helps the people around you get a little bit braver, too.

HELEN: In the summer of 2014, I needed a lot of help to see that my going 'all in', as Kate explained, was actually me showing strength; it definitely didn't feel like it! Emotionally and mentally, I was on the brink. Well, actually I'd fallen over the edge, and I didn't know how to pull myself out. I knew I wanted to get out, but I also knew I couldn't do it alone. By chance, I stumbled across a TED Talk on 'The Power of Vulnerability'.[1] The speaker, Brené Brown, who has now become something of a guru for me, spoke right to the core of my soul. Her words resonated so much they reverberated through

---

[1] Brené Brown's TED talk is available at: www.ted.com/talks/brene_brown_the_power_of_vulnerability?language=en (last accessed 17 March 2021).

my entire body. As she spoke, the tears that had been rolling down my face started to dry up, I became lighter with every word she uttered, and I could see more clearly than I had ever done before.

I started to understand that the only thing I had done 'wrong' was to give my whole self to something. Exactly nine weeks before selection for the 2014 World Cup, I underwent surgery on my back. It was my second back surgery for a ruptured disc in less than a year. When I look back now and think about what I was hoping to achieve, it does seem a tad crazy. I was already in a very fragile state of mind because of the constant back pain and lack of sleep, but I couldn't *not* give it a go. I'd already given 16 years of my life to this team and I had a dream of becoming a world champion, and this would be my last chance. I didn't ever want to wonder, 'What if?' So I went for it. I gave every last ounce of energy I had for nine solid weeks, from recovery to rehabilitation and, eventually, full-blown training. I was amazed at my progress. I even made it onto the pitch and played in a friendly match versus China. I felt I was ready. The coach didn't agree.

I had jumped out of a plane, and when I read the selection email, my parachute didn't open. Everything that I knew to be true in my world felt like it was in ruins, and my ego and I were left in tatters. Although I was in so much pain, I can now appreciate that this pain was my only option. I could have played it safe and not even attempted to get fit for the World Cup, but then my chance of being selected would have been zero. Even if I did need help to see this, I started to accept that it was the act of trying that was courageous, regardless of the outcome.

My struggle still continued for some time. Bit by bit, I had to dismantle the vulnerability barricade I'd surrounded myself with in order to hide the real me. It's funny how the term 'defence mechanism' is reasonably common in everyday language and something we recognise in others, and yet our own defence mechanisms are something very few of us will actually talk about. My number-one go-to is to shut down. Even though I am craving connection, my natural reaction is to destroy any chance of that happening by not letting anyone in. I eventually realised that the only way out was to give into what I was feeling, and to acknowledge the pain. I had to name it and, importantly, let go of how I thought my life should be or how I wanted it to be. I needed the courage to be imperfect, and I had to share it. So I did. In fits and starts, I gradually spoke my truth, which in turn, thankfully, was reciprocated with love, empathy and connection from those around me who truly mattered. Over the following months and even years, I have accepted that that experience was actually when I felt most alive. It has allowed me to connect with people on a completely different level, from a place of deep empathy, and for that I am truly grateful.

If we want our employees, colleagues and friends to take risks, to give their all, to be creative and innovative in order to produce something amazing, we have to allow for the whole host of vulnerabilities that come with that. That means two things. First, you have to create safe spaces where people can open up and share all of what they're thinking and feeling. We don't know when someone might be feeling vulnerable, so it needs to be a constant thing. As we suggested in the previous chapter, this has to start with the leaders, but we all have a role to play in the language we use and the reactions we have to someone speaking their truth or giving their all. Second, remember that we are human. And when humans feel vulnerable, our defence mechanisms will sometimes kidnap our better judgement. They may even try to sabotage relationships. There is normally a reason for why someone might be acting out or behaving in a way you don't like, so, if you can – and I know this can be hard – stay curious: they just might need your help.

What vulnerability is not

KATE: I was sitting in the changing room in Rio before our warm-up for the final against the Dutch and I realised I was starting to get a migraine. Before the debilitating headache and nausea kick in, I get an early onset of aura; my vision gets progressively blurry and it's like having flashing stars everywhere I look. This, I knew, was not the time to be showing vulnerability to the whole team. We were about to play in an Olympic final and everyone was going through their pre-game mental routines. The last thing I wanted was to shift this focus. So, I quietly confided in Helen, Alex Danson, the physio and our doctor. I took some medication and lay down in the back part of the changing room. Fortunately for me, when I catch my migraines this early, with medication, I tend to be able to function fully without the rest of the symptoms showing up. I played the game, and none of my teammates, aside from Helen and Alex, would ever have known. I had to be mindful about my intentions for sharing in that moment and recognise who were the appropriate people to tell – I needed to get medication quickly and ensure plan B was ready to go if it came to the worst and I was unable to play my normal role as captain, without disrupting the team.

Vulnerability isn't about sharing everything of yourself, with everybody, always – particularly if, in doing so, it would compromise your desired outcome. Being completely open to all of my teammates in that instance could have upset our preparation and focus. Choosing to share the fact I had a migraine and any potential fears I may have been experiencing with some key players and staff allowed me to be vulnerable in a managed way – one that was best for me and the team. Being vulnerable, then, is about sharing your thoughts, emotions and feelings in a way that sits authentically with you. In this way, we must all set our own boundaries for each situation in which we find ourselves. If all that you can share is that you are not comfortable in sharing, that in itself is you being vulnerable. It is brave to say I'm not comfortable with this, to share how you are feeling and what you are thinking in an open and honest way.

Trust

KATE: I genuinely believe from having seen and experienced it myself that vulnerability is a connective force. And connection impacts performance. As Patrick Lencioni illustrates in his book *The Five Dysfunctions of a Team: A Leadership Fable*, a team that is unwilling to be vulnerable is likely to have an absence of trust, and without trust a team cannot function at a consistently high level. When our psychologist, Tom Cross, prompted us to share what helped and hindered our performance with our teammates on camp in San Diego, it was a revelation. One player's story was a game changer for me. This particular player spoke openly about how what I shouted to her on the pitch was having a massive negative impact on her performance and mental state. She knew I meant well but would prefer that I took a different tack with her. I felt it all: emotional for her and the detrimental effect I'd been having on her; shame and embarrassment for myself. For a fully signed-up member to the 'people pleasing' club like me, this was a huge kick of reality.

One person's sharing of their truth not only increased our empathy and understanding for her but also made us all look inwardly at ourselves and our own truths. It was even more impactful from the team perspective, strengthening our connection. I know that when someone is prepared to open themselves up and share in that way there is an innate need in all of us to care for that person. When someone lays their soul bare for us in this way, we are compelled to open ourselves up, too, and that's the magic of the vulnerability loop. It is self-feeding, self-nourishing and, for a team, life altering. We may not ever be best of friends, but the trust and respect will remain for life. If you have deemed me worthy enough to see all of you and you have allowed me space to share all of me, we are great teammates and we are on our way to being a great team.

I think that, in almost all the teams I've played on internationally, there was an unspoken acknowledgement that, while we might not all be best friends, we could function at a high level professionally for the good of the team. Having a shared team purpose, of course, aids this alignment as does the sharing of some or all personal values. This depth of connection can sustain a good team. But for a team to really excel I think there has to be another level of sharing and that comes from within each of us. Being vulnerable to any degree within a team takes courage, and for some it is a huge leap of faith, but the payback is immeasurable. The empathy and care are contagious; it is empowering and inspirational. To witness one of your teammates being bold enough to express their innermost thoughts and feelings demands your engagement and complete attention.

When you open up and allow people in to see all of you, it is more likely that in turn your teammates will honour you with their truth. If you can create space for your team to share strengths and weaknesses, triumphs and failures, you are creating a solid foundation of trust for your culture to thrive upon. Where there is honesty and trust, your people are more likely to give it their all and take responsibility for driving the team culture towards your end goal. And this is how vulnerability ultimately affects performance: it creates strong connections between people and cements your joint purpose. This is the gold dust.

HELEN: It also provides us with knowledge – really important knowledge about our teammates and colleagues that can help them perform better. Who wouldn't want that? This can actually be useful to keep in mind, especially if you're someone that finds opening up more challenging than others. Giving yourself to vulnerability is definitely not easy to do. It can be a long process and constantly evolves over time, so go easy on yourself. A good place to start is to think about feedback. Feedback helps everyone, and even though giving and receiving feedback can be equally hard, by making it a consistent practice it can help lower the guards we tend to put up over time. It's also a great way for leaders to show the way and allow themselves to be open to feeling vulnerable in front of their team. There is no better way to show that a space is safe.

During the London 2012 Olympic cycle we put a regular review meeting in the diary, every few months or so. Because we were starting our full-time programme for the first time, and from scratch, it was imperative that we learned lessons along the way. The players and staff broke off into small groups, and going through every aspect of our programme we considered if there was anything we needed to 'start' doing, what needed to 'stop', and what was going well and needed to 'continue'. Start, stop, continue – it's a well-known process, and we made so many improvements by doing it. I could also see how hard it was at times, in particular for the staff and especially our coach, Danny. That was where most of the feedback was directed, purely because they're the ones holding the power. It would have been so easy to take the comments personally and meet our demands with short, sharp nos. But they didn't; they tried incredibly hard to remain open to what we were saying for the good of the team.

It was a win-win. The staff gathered knowledge from what we were thinking as a group of players, and we felt listened to and valued. The amount of trust and respect that I had for Danny and the staff certainly grew in those sessions as well. What's important to recognise is that being vulnerable isn't always about sharing parts of yourself. Equally as challenging for most of us, or even harder for some, is being open to hear what others think about you and how you're doing things. Many of you will view the process of receiving feedback as an attack on your ego. Essentially, that is exactly what receiving challenging feedback feels like in the moment. It touches a nerve, and we feel it in all manner of ways, but we certainly feel it. Even with clearly laid-out boundaries and an assurance of some level of control it is difficult. But it is necessary that we listen to and understand our reactions because they reveal so much about us as people. Only when we accept our thoughts can we understand our feelings and take full control of how we proceed with the information that has been presented. Yes, it's hard, but we can do hard things. Choosing to ask for feedback and allowing yourself to be vulnerable can provide infinite growth for you and your team.

KATE: There's one important proviso, though: vulnerability should never be forced upon you. In order to get the benefits of sharing the deepest parts of ourselves, it has to be done willingly. I feel strongly about this, having experienced both methods. In 2014, when I was at an emotional and mental breaking point, I was singled out in a meeting by my teammates, as were a couple of other players. I do not necessarily disagree with the things that were said to me in that meeting; it was, after all, what the players felt and it was how I had been making them feel. Indeed, it might have been powerful if we'd had an open sharing of where we all were individually at that time. Instead, I felt as though I'd been thrust under the interrogation spotlight without warning, and I broke. In fairness, I was already broken, worn down by months of enduring the toxic culture that had become entrenched in the group I was leading.

One player specifically took the opportunity to point the finger of blame at me. I don't hold this against her; in fact, she remains one of my closest friends. I don't remember everything that was said to me, but I do remember the opening line: 'We've lost you.' She was dead right: they had lost me. I had checked out emotionally in the hope of preserving some little corner of myself. I felt under attack, under siege. Everything I had learned and experienced was telling me that this was not right, that this culture, this team environment, this leadership style was wrong. I was screaming inside and almost silent on the outside, save for a couple of very unsavoury outbursts. And yet here I was in this 'circle of trust' feeling no trust at all. What was once a safe space for me became completely unsafe. Here was someone *forcing* me to be vulnerable by opening up, and it almost cost me everything. Therapy and support from close friends and an enormous amount of love and understanding from Helen helped me stay afloat. I learned a great deal about myself and about the power of vulnerability. And the most important lesson was this: that when I choose when and how much I share about myself, we all grow; but that when you choose for me, we all lose. Trust is broken, respect is broken, and all must be rebuilt from the ground up.

If you have ever had trust broken by someone close to you, you know that it can feel like there will never be trust again. Trust can be lost in an instant and take years to get back. But, it can be rebuilt, piece by piece and moment by moment. It must start from a place of honesty and total candidness, and with at least one person willing to start the process of reassembling the connection. I understand that this breaking of trust and lack of respect for your vulnerability is a very real fear which prevents many of you from sharing yourself to any degree with the people you work with. For some of you, sharing is the easiest thing in the world and you will happily share everything and anything about yourself. Others of you are more reserved and careful with your sharing. Both approaches are perfectly normal, and both can exist in one team. Part of the point of vulnerability is that it's yours to own and yours to share. What we really want you to take away from this chapter is that whatever level feels right to you, it's worth it – the uncomfortable moments and hard work of owning your vulnerability and sharing it with those around you can create more fulfilment and joy, which can in turn lead to improved performance.

We believe there's something innate in all human beings that when someone opens up to us and makes themselves vulnerable, we want to support and care for that person. The same can be said about being open and truly honest with ourselves, too. When we connect at a deep level with ourselves and others, we find belonging and trust, love and empathy. All of these things help us win together. Fostering deep levels of trust takes time; building great team culture takes time. We've been amazed at how many corporations have confessed to us over the years that they don't want to take time away from the day job to work on culture. To which we always respond: culture is the day job.

With the start of our centralised programme came more time. We could spend time together in the gym, on the pitch, doing group work, meeting up for coffee and maybe even going down to the local pub quiz together. We talked to one another about our lives, we shared in one another's triumphs and disasters. In short, we became completely invested in one another's lives. As we have stated, this did not make us best friends, but we genuinely cared about these people, all of them. And this is where trust lives and where good culture thrives. In the next chapter we will share the tools we used that helped foster vulnerability in our team and build trust one moment at a time.

Team huddle

Truly great teams are connected. They are connected by purpose and they are connected by something even deeper, their vulnerability. Teams that have environments which foster authentic sharing of self will help you feel like you belong because you will feel seen and accepted. Here are some things to try and to consider when opening up to your own vulnerability and that of your team.

Questions to consider

- What has been your experience of going 'all in'?
- When do you feel at your most vulnerable?
- How does your body react and what do you notice about your thoughts, feelings and behaviours when you are vulnerable?
- How much do you really know about the people that you work with, and how much do they know about you?
- Are you open to feedback and how do you react when you receive it?

Key team tactics

- Be brave.
- Lead by example – by you showing your vulnerability, it gives the green light to everyone else in the group. Being prepared to show you don't have all the answers is a nice example of this.
- Asking for direct and honest feedback makes you vulnerable as a leader. Regular 'start, stop and continue' reviews with various people will demonstrate a willingness to face the vulnerability and work through it for the good of the team.

- When someone opens up at any level, be respectful of what they are bestowing on you. Be mindful of this gift and be firm with those wanting to turn personal stories into idle gossip.
- Do some of the exercises we talk about in Chapter 7, on awareness.
- Explore the use of personality-profiling tools or development plans to begin the process of sharing vulnerability to a level that people feel comfortable with.
- Moments of team vulnerability come through shared experiences. Provide different types of interactive sessions where day-to-day roles and responsibilities are changed or altered.
- If there is a lack of vulnerability in your team, facilitate conversations around the safeness of the space or environment, and work together to create understanding around the role everyone can play in making it feel safe for everyone.

7

Awareness

In some ways this might be the most impactful chapter of the book. Awareness is certainly one of the areas that resonates most with people when we're speaking to different organisations and teams. While a focus on culture, vulnerability and leadership are all vital to any individual or team wanting to function at a high level, none of that can be addressed without awareness.

Take the dictionary definition of awareness – 'knowledge that something exists'[1] – and then consider what it means to be self-aware and aware of others. To appreciate my existence, I need to know myself fully. To appreciate your existence, I need to know you in the same way. As Eckhart Tolle has said: 'Awareness is the greatest agent for change.'[2] When we are able to step away from ourselves and see who we are, how we think, feel and behave, then we can make changes because we can see the changes we need to make.

Awareness leads us to our authentic selves and to authentic relationships with others. We have spent a great deal of time in the last few years of our sporting career holding up a metaphorical mirror to our faces and taking a good long hard stare. With the support of our team psychologists, we did some work that without doubt helped us as performers but which, most importantly, helped us as people.

In this chapter we will explore the exercises that we used as athletes to deepen the connection with ourselves and with one another. This is inextricably linked to vulnerability (the subject of the previous chapter), and so it demands honesty, bravery and courage. You will find things that you

---

[1] Definition taken from Cambridge Dictionary, available at: https://dictionary.cambridge.org/dictionary/english/awareness (Last accessed 21 March 2021)

[2] Tolle, Eckhart, *A New Earth: Create a Better Life* (Penguin, 2009)

absolutely love about yourself, but also, probably, things that you don't. Both are useful, because the very fact that you can see anything at all means that you exist, you are aware, and you can now really begin to thrive.

Playing to your super strengths

HELEN: If you had to say out loud right now one thing that you're exceptional at, or that you love about yourself, would you be able to do so straight away?

On the other hand, if you were asked to name all the things that you hate about yourself, or that you're not very good at, do they come to mind a bit quicker?

Be honest.

When we ask these two questions during our talks and workshops, in the main we get a quizzical look for the first one, maybe a few shakes of the head. The second one, on the other hand, is greeted with nods of recognition. As a team that's exactly where we were. It's crazy when you think about it: we were the GB hockey team, as individuals we were the very best at what we did in the whole country, and, remarkably, we either didn't know what our strengths were, or we weren't prepared to say them out loud.

This isn't surprising when you examine the academic research into this area. Historically, improvement and development have been about identifying gaps, focusing on correcting what's wrong rather than considering what's done well and leveraging on that. This is beginning to change, as strength-based approaches are being shown to be fruitful: recognising your team's strengths can make a difference to future success by generating higher engagement and motivation to replicate these positive behaviours and results. This is exactly what happened to us. Kate and I had been playing for our country for over a decade before we properly identified our individual strengths and actually used them to the benefit of the team. The difference was remarkable. Adding *strengths* – good qualities –

and *super strengths* – exceptional qualities – to our language and approach was motivating; it was exciting and it was something we wanted to be a part of.

Knowing and owning your personal strengths is important for a number of reasons. Your strengths are your value. They're your worth. They're what you can positively bring to the team. Having absolute clarity and certainty surrounding this can and should be matched against your role. Now you know your role, and you know that it plays to your strengths, you can deliver it with absolute authority and confidence. Imagine being able to look around at every single member of your team knowing everyone is doing the same. Creating a culture that encourages everyone to play to their strengths also helps us to appreciate others, as well as be appreciated ourselves – feeling valued is essential for any human being.

Speaking and sharing our strengths was really at the core of where the difference was made. It was hard – possibly harder than we were anticipating. Don't be fooled by the seemingly positive slant of acknowledging our strengths; it still makes us incredibly vulnerable because of the one question most of us will probably ask ourselves – what if others don't agree?

We all showed a lot of bravery by doing this work, and for me personally it was a game changer during the penalty shootout in the Olympic final in Rio. As I stepped forward to take the penalty stroke, I went through all of the processes I had learned over the years, and subsequently practised time after time for hours back at our training base. Yes, I felt prepared for that moment because of all the physical and mental practice I had undertaken, but I was also confident I could deliver what I needed to because I knew my strengths and I knew that others knew them, too.

As a hockey player, one of my strengths was my basic skills, something I'd been drilling since my early days of holding a stick. Under fatigue and pressure my basic skills rarely let me down. As I made that long walk up to the spot and placed the ball in position, I was confident in myself. But there was something more important. Because we had had the courage to share our strengths, I knew that all of my teammates who stood on the halfway line wouldn't have wanted anyone else taking that penalty other than me. Now, to know that in that moment was incredibly powerful. Regardless of the outcome, my team trusted me to do my job, and this lifted me up and gave me all the strength I needed to deliver.

The beauty of it is that we *all* have that power. We are all capable of lifting up our teammates and colleagues, our friends and our family, by telling them what they're good at. When we explored our own strengths and shared them with the group, we invariably missed loads of great positives about ourselves, simply because we weren't aware of them. Next time a colleague makes you feel good about yourself, or helps you to perform better, or is a great person to talk to – whatever it is – find some courage and tell them! Lift up those around you, and it will circle back around in no time, leaving you to wonder why you never did it before.

Celebrating everyone's contributions

HELEN: Not only did we work on our individual strengths, we also discussed the team's super strengths, and how we all had a role to play in implementing that. Identifying our core game always meant that, whatever situation we faced in a game and however we were playing, we knew that our foundation was rock solid and we could always rely on that. Indecision and ambiguity are where things can go wrong. When everyone knows the plan, how to execute it and their role within that plan, once again it means you can deliver it with authority and confidence.

The process of identifying our strengths and establishing our core game meant, rather than wasting energy on trying to be something we weren't, we leveraged on our unique blend of strengths. When you have a squad of 31 and a staff group covering all areas of expertise you soon start to realise that there's not a huge amount you haven't got covered anyway and that how you harness those strengths, regardless of who's providing them, is the key. Having and knowing the varied strengths in your team will allow for different people to step up and take the lead when that specific strength is required, enhancing your chances of a successful outcome.

It was also vital that everyone's strengths were valued equally. Not one contribution is better than another. However, in many walks of life, and definitely within sport, that can get very lost. The press and media, sponsors, fans, even our association at times, constantly and consistently celebrate the contribution of some players – for example the goal scorers or the captain – above that of others. It's inevitable, and it happens all the time in every sport. I would also argue that it happens on a daily basis in *all* team settings. There's no getting away from that external gaze and praise, but *you* can take control of how *you* view things. Yes, you need someone to lead that pitch, but you also need that other person who spent hour upon hour doing background research and due diligence on the client. The reason we won gold was because we covered all the bases and because there were people willing to give their heart and soul to their role knowing full well they wouldn't get the plaudits from anyone other than the team. It takes the whole team to achieve a team goal. Acknowledging and celebrating every contribution, however small, is imperative.

Good day, bad day

KATE: If knowing and owning our super strengths is fundamental to us being able to be our best selves, then being mindful enough to see the good and the bad in real time will enable you to be your best self more often. Good days and bad days, we all have them. They affect how we think, feel and behave, and therefore how we perform. In the GB hockey team we needed to perform as a group and as individuals whether it was a good day or not, and on all the so-so days in between. If anyone has ever experienced a negative spiral where a bad moment becomes a bad morning, a bad day and a bad week, you'll know how debilitating this can be. We wanted to try to shorten these moments and, if possible, stop them in their infancy. We also wanted to flourish and find ways to 'do' as many good days as possible.

We worked through the following 'Good Day/Bad Day' exercise with our psychologist, Dr Andrea Furst, before Rio. It certainly sounds easy enough, but to be honest it was some of the hardest work I've done on myself. The real magic here lies not just in seeing what happens to you when you're 'doing' a good day or a bad day, but also what happens when you move between these two states. Being able to recognise what shifts you from a good day to a bad one can be the key that unlocks your ability to perform consistently well and also be well doing it.

With this exercise there is first of all a need for stillness and reflection. You have to consider what happens to you mentally, physically and emotionally when you're doing a good day and a bad day. What is your body language like? How do people see you? The kind of day you're doing is shown even in the clothes you choose to wear that day. (For example, you'll see me with my hood up when I'm doing a bad day; it's my way of retreating from the world.) Does the tone of your voice change? How about how you interact with people? Is that the same? What does your internal voice sound like when you're doing a good or bad day? I know that, on a bad day, my internal voice can be either like a Tasmanian devil or a whispering ghost, but on a good one it's assured and serene. How do you feel on a good day or bad day, and what impact does this have on you?

Be honest.

The only way to work through any of this is with absolute, total, brutal honesty. You have to face up to not how you think you are, not what you'd like others to think about you, but the realness of you.

This was hard for me. For a very long time I was very busy making it look as though everything was good to the outside world, even when it was the very opposite of good. I thought this was what leadership was about. This is what other leaders had taught me. I had become so accustomed to this game that I had lost the ability to really feel what I was feeling. To change this, I had to put in a lot of time and energy to assess what my days were really like. How was today? How was I? Where was I? What did all of this look and feel like to me?

So here is *my* honest account of myself. My good days see me engaged and present. My mind works quickly and calmly. I love to be around people and interact with people. I am emotive and that's OK. I like fixing things and helping people, and this gives me energy. I like to multitask and be busy. On the other side of the coin, when I do a bad day, I really do one! I want to withdraw from the world. My thoughts are either wildly frantic or eerily still. My emotions are all over the place, and woe betide anyone I come into contact with. I take on too much and try to do everything. I am in full control freak mode, and everyone around me just has to hold on tight and wait for the storm to pass. I still feel a bit queasy typing this out. Even now, this honest self-assessment is tough to take.

Once you have had an honest look at yourself, then you can begin the magical work, exploring your triggers. What shifts you from a good day into a bad day? It can be very specific, a range of things or an accumulation of things that together form the perfect storm. For me it is a perfectly imperfect storm of tiredness, feeling useless, vulnerable or under attack, and wanting to be all things to all people. This sends me off to a place that I don't want to be and is really hard to get out of once I'm there. So my work, for the rest of my days, is to try to stay mindful enough to notice when these triggers might show up, or when they have already turned up and are running wild! I know I need to give myself some time to rest and recharge my energy stores. It is OK in this moment to acknowledge that I have low energy and that I need the wonderful people around me to carry some of my load for a time. To use their strengths will help me be strong.

If you are able to do this work and are prepared to carry on doing it, you will do more good days than bad. You will prevent bad moments from spiralling into bad weeks. You will have a greater connection with yourself and those around you. In the GB hockey team we ensured this was the case because we shared our honest self-reflections with one another. For some players this came easily; for others it was more challenging. We needed to be understanding of our differences and be mindful not to judge. We spent almost every day together, many of us had shared various big life moments away from the hockey pitch, and we'd seen each other at our best and worst. We were encouraged to talk openly and honestly in meetings. People's opinions were sought and actively listened to. We created a circle of trust both physically and metaphorically as we pulled our chairs into a circle and listened to one another.

Will everyone share all of themselves in your team? Possibly not, and that's OK. What is vital is that you have a group of influential leaders who are actively engaged in the processes of self-reflection, self-perception and self-correction. They also need to be willing to share openly and honestly with the team. Many of you reading this may be thinking that internal competition for promotions and bonuses will prevent this work from happening in your team. We were also in direct competition with one another and yet we shared deeply because we had total faith in our culture. You must trust yourself and one another with this precious information. You must promise never to use what is shared for personal gain or mockery. This is for your team and no one else. In listening to one another's truth with a non-judgemental ear you are showing that you care about these people and you are invested in them being their best self. That is teamwork.

The state of you

HELEN: We all want to have as many 'good' days as possible, and when it comes to being able to perform a specific task at a very specific moment, we need to be at our best for that, too. For us that specific moment was every match, every tournament and even every training session. For you that might be a job interview, making a pitch or giving a speech, or it might be that you, too, need to 'perform' every single day just like us. Cultivating the 'right' state of mind in order to approach situations where you need to perform is a skill, and it takes practice. Our psychologists used to tell us that your brain is a muscle: you train your muscles, and therefore you must also train your brain. There is no magic fix; it takes time and consistency for our muscles to get stronger, and the same is true of our brain. Andrea called this optimal state of mind our 'performance mindset'. With her guidance and through practice it helped us to automatically produce thoughts and emotions that were productive, and its aim was for us to consistently produce our A game.

In terms of performance, we are all seeking consistency at an optimal level. If every individual in your team was able to control all that they can in terms of mental, physical and emotional readiness, then just think where your team could take this combined effort. Of course, we can't control everything and there needs to be flexibility and agility built into this work. However, by focusing on what we can do, on how we feel, on how we ready ourselves, we are giving ourselves the best chance to deliver as best we can on any given day.

As important as it is to know your A game, you must also know your 'Z game' inside out. We often want to gloss over our worst performances as quickly as possible and move on. Actually, by taking the time to unpick them a little bit we can begin to notice triggers that start us sliding away from our A game. This sense of self-mastery and control is hugely powerful to have to hand when in a high-pressure and uncertain environment.

When you're learning something new, it can often feel clunky and robotic. But with practice you can become proficient at making small adjustments that can have a huge impact on performance – it'll feel like turning the thermostat up or down by point one of a degree. Halfway through my career I integrated a moment of pause into my pre-game ritual where I did just that. After our physical warm-up and before I picked up my stick, I spent a couple of minutes sitting on the bench by myself. I would ask myself, 'Where am I?' If I wasn't in the right spot, I would tend to be in one of two places – dispassionate or nervous as hell. If I was feeling detached, I learned that an array of emotions got me into the right place: gratitude, pride, passion or even anger. Being thankful for the experience I was having, and to those that helped me get there, or angry for those who didn't have the same opportunities as me, seemed to do the trick. I would literally think about my family or about the injustices in the world and the emotions would start to flow. If I was nervous, I simply acknowledged my fear as normal and then I'd remind myself that the worst thing that could happen is we could lose, and that's not the end of the world (even though deep down I would think it was!).

It's a process and you're going to get it wrong to begin with, but trial and error is actually a good way to progress with this. Speaking to colleagues and friends also works: what do they see when you're performing well? How can they help you get there? How do they get to their A game and is there anything you can learn from them? We really don't need to do this work by ourselves. So persevere and keep going. I can't say this often enough: take notice of the state you're in and think about where you need to be, and then figure out what you need to do to get there.

Getting out of your comfort zone

KATE: Sometimes work and life can feel like Groundhog Day. This can feel draining or you may find solace in the routine. But what happens to you when you're thrown a curve ball or are thrust into a new position and new territory? Life is becoming more and more uncertain, and we all need to adapt more quickly and become more agile. In order to not only cope but thrive in such turbulent circumstances we must regularly throw ourselves into the unknown and the uncomfortable. This is not a new concept, and you will have likely already taken part in such activities on numerous occasions in the form of team-building awaydays!

To be frank with you, I shudder at the mere sight of those two words together – 'team building'. The fear of wasting time and of being thrust into the spotlight as I get 'tested' in front of my peers is not that appealing, to be honest. However, we as a women's hockey team were no different from any corporate team: we needed a smattering of organised days during which we were taken out of our comfort zone. Although every day of training was one big team-building exercise, it was important that we undertook something completely different now and again. The natural hierarchies and order of things that exist in every group were part of our training environment and needed to be shaken up. Only when we are forced to take on a different role can perspectives be shifted; after all, one person's comfort zone is another person's hell on earth.

For us, where better to start being taken out of our comfort zones than at the Royal Marines training base in Lympstone, Devon? It was hell. It was useful, and it really helped. And it was also hell. The Marines broke us down to our base level mentally, physically and emotionally, and then it started. We were split into strategic groups and asked to perform tasks. We had to lead and be led in situations that were alien to all of us. Individuals were being asked to execute orders that felt uncomfortable and confronting. We were being challenged at every level, and it was really tough. Although we learned a lot about ourselves and our teammates over the course of these three days, it was this last punishing exercise on the final day that made us all feel so proud of our team. We competed in two groups as we fought to complete a long, arduous military-style operation which saw us pushed far beyond the limits of what we thought we were capable. We brought each other home that day, and we drew on that experience in future tournaments when we were challenged in a similar vein on the hockey pitch.

It can't all be about physical exertion and strategic thinking, though; we are different and we need to be stressed in different ways and across a range of environments. For us, if the Royal Marines was at one end of the spectrum, then perhaps the other end was provided by improvisational comedy! We had the wonderful Neil Mullarkey come in and teach us the basics of improv. There's no script, and you have to think, move and respond quickly. There are skills and techniques that make comedy work, just as there are in hockey and probably in your line of work, too. In moments of pressure, it's important that you are mindful of your physical, emotional and psychological responses. Can you perform the skills and think clearly when you are feeling at your most challenged and most pressured?

At times, people in your team will need mental or physical support. At times you will need that same support. Together, you can find a way. To get the most out of these 'awaydays' you must reflect on them often, remember what you've learned, and think how you will use this growth to move towards your goal. To move past the frustration of taking time away from the day job, make sure it is absolutely about your day job. Comfort zones can be hugely reassuring but there is no growth there. By embracing the discomfort of challenge together you will be more able to push towards your vision as a team.

Mindful in the moment

HELEN: The team awaydays helped us understand what happens to us under the pressure we faced within those situations. It was a starting point for real growth in all of our awareness levels. To make those days, as well as the exercises we did with our psychologists, worthwhile, we needed to relate whatever we learned back to the day job as much as we could, and that for us was playing hockey. If you don't do this part, whatever insights you gain will likely be wasted. As soon as you're back at work and the pressure starts to build, your old habits will probably return very quickly. Just because you now know that you get angry when you're pushed, or defensive when you're questioned, or do everything yourself when time is short doesn't mean you'll stop reacting that way – unless you take conscious steps to make it so. It takes time, and it requires you to be mindful.

We were pushed, questioned and challenged on the pitch all the time – no more so than in the 'Thinking Thursday' session we talked about in Chapter 4. It was physically tough, so it was often the hardest session of the week. We were tested mentally on our knowledge of tactics and philosophy, and our ability to adapt quickly to last-minute changes. Our coaches deliberately facilitated chaos when we were under extreme fatigue so that we could practise managing any emotions that might end up being harmful to our success on the pitch. You won't need to manufacture stress like we needed to; life is already pretty good at doing that for most of us. Deadlines, structural changes, reviews, internal promotions, bereavements, last-minute childcare issues, random flat tyres, even global pandemics! And all when you're utterly exhausted.

Learning to be mindful and in the present moment is your key to conscious change. First, you must notice the emotion. Then pause. This gap is gold dust. It's where the work is done, and it's where you have the chance to change your reaction from an old habit to whatever you now want it to be. In the women's hockey team, we would help one another out with appropriate reminders, and sharing our 'areas to improve' kept us all accountable. It also meant that, when we messed up and old habits crept back in, there was more understanding, empathy and compassion because everyone knew we were doing our best in that moment.

A very important point of note is that this work isn't about making wholesale changes to your personality; that's not possible, and it wouldn't be good for your mental health anyway. It's more about being able to see the parts of us that maybe don't always get the best out of ourselves and those around us, accepting them as part of us, and then, instead of saying, 'Well, this is me, like it or lump it,' trying to figure out a way of making it work for everyone. On the pitch I was someone who could get angry at times. By practising various strategies, I learned that the worst thing I could do was to eliminate that anger altogether, which just made me numb and dampened my strengths as a player. Instead, the best strategy for me was to accept it and channel it. That way, I kept the fight in me while remaining calm enough to make clear decisions and communicate in a way that would always benefit the team. It also allowed me to notice, sometimes with the help of others, when my anger started to boil over. If you don't make time to accept the parts of you that aren't always helpful, when you make a mistake – as we all will at some point – it leaves a space for frustration and recrimination to creep in and exacerbate your emotions even more.

From a team perspective the most helpful strategy we found was to remain task-focused. Keeping your goal front of mind allows people to simply concentrate on doing their job. When these are aligned with your strengths, as discussed above, then even better. Kate and I and many of our Rio teammates commented on how mindful we were both on and off the pitch during the Olympics itself. We were so in the moment, it felt almost eerie. By taking one game at a time (there's a lot of truth in the old sporting clichés), and thinking only of the game plan and the role we all needed to play within that, we did not give our minds a chance to think about anything else other than delivering what we needed to deliver.

The work in this chapter is as much about self-acceptance as it is about self-awareness. First, we must be aware, and then we can begin to accept. Only when we have a 'warts and all' understanding of who we truly are and how we respond to changes in circumstance can we begin to grow as people. Much of this work can be done without spending any money, though all of this work will require you spending time. Often, we think that spending time on ourselves can feel and appear selfish. This is not only wrong, it is also harmful and stifles our potential as human beings. As leaders, you must build reflection time into your work schedule and treat it with the respect and seriousness it requires. Be protective of these moments of growth: used wisely they can take your people and your culture to the next level.

There can be no better way to affect behaviour change than by role-modelling exactly what you need to see from those around you. Be brave, be candid and be vulnerable. Create your own circles of trust and guard them and their contents with your life. You will find this tough; this is hard work, after all. Being truly self-aware demands you to be patient and kind to yourself. Having an awareness of others will demand you to be patient and kind to them. All of this will enable you to live more mindfully. When we are connected with ourselves, we can connect so much more meaningfully with the people around us, be they teammates, colleagues, friends or family.

All of the work on awareness in this chapter leads on neatly to the work on challenge and conflict in the next chapter. To leverage on the transformative power of honest challenge, we must first have a foundation of trust built from awareness, acceptance and vulnerability.

Team huddle

Awareness is a lifelong journey and will require empathy, kindness and understanding. The return on investment will be life changing as you will experience greater levels of fulfilment, and so this work is more than worth your time and dedication. Increasing awareness of yourself and others will help you be more mindful and fully present in each moment as well. In a team setting this will lead to clearer decisions, better connectivity and deep levels of trust.

Questions to consider

- Are you living true to yourself?
- How well do you know the people around you?
- What value do you bring to your team?
- What do you value in other people?
- What kind of person do you want to be today and how will you make that happen?
- What happens to you under pressure?
- When negative thoughts and emotions arise, how do you deal with them?

Key team tactics

- We all need to own our strengths. Being comfortable with owning your super strengths will allow you to thrive and be resilient. They will change and adapt as you grow, but they will always remain the essence of you. Think and reflect on them often. Be prepared to ask others for their opinion but know that it's your opinion that matters most.
- Sharing your individual strengths within a team is a wonderful exercise. Creating a safe space to do so takes time, but this is a good way to bring vulnerability to the group in a positive way. Not only will it create good

team energy, it will also allow you to see your differences and increase your ability to leverage on this difference towards your collective vision.

- Doing the 'Good Day/Bad Day' exercise will take time and a fair bit of breaking through to an uncomfortable place. You will need to remain open and curious. Once you are able to assess where you are mentally and emotionally without judgement, you will be well on the way to being able to do more good days than bad.

- To find your A game you first have to identify a time when you feel you were performing or being the best version of yourself. Being able to remember what that looked like, felt like and sounded like means that you're already closer to recreating it. Review and reflect often to maximise your understanding of where you need to be and how to get there mentally, physically and emotionally.

- Pushing people out of their comfort zones in a safe space can unlock potential in your people and your team. For example, experiment with changing roles in team meetings. If there is someone who always gives the most input, make them be silent for a designated period. If you would like to hear more from certain people, make them team leader for the session. There is great growth potential when we navigate challenge in team environments.

8

Challenge and conflict

Why would we have a chapter based solely around conflict and challenge? After all, conflict is bad, right? Well, yes and no! First, in an environment that is built to support, and almost demand, conflict and challenge, they can really shift team performance and create forward momentum. However, the environment must be a safe one and the skills of the people within the team must be well honed and developed in terms of both giving and receiving challenge. It would be much easier and far more comfortable to avoid friction entirely and just go with the flow. But as we've repeatedly hammered home in this book, nothing is gained from living in your comfort zone. Growth for you and your team lies in being open to contradictory ideas and new ways of tackling problems.

What images or thoughts are conjured up when you see the words 'conflict' and 'challenge'? How we have been raised to view disagreement and direct feedback shapes how perturbed we are by them. More often than not, we view these as negative aspects of team life or work life, and that's understandable – we all want an easier life. In this chapter, however, we hope to demonstrate, through our experiences of using conflict and challenge in a sporting environment, how, if embraced by all, they can be positive tools for change, improving both individual and team performance. For clarity, we define conflict and challenge as productive ideological conversations around ideas and concepts that can be passionate and emotional. Only when we embrace conflict and diversity of thought, experience and opinion can we ever truly build teams and environments where everyone belongs. And, crucially, moments of friction when harnessed and worked through can be catalysts for magical metamorphosis.

The necessary foundation

KATE: Challenging environments where people are holding themselves and each other to account should be something we all want to be a part of. If we are surrounding ourselves with diverse perspectives and differing opinions, conflict cannot be avoided, and nor should it, in our opinion. However, the vast majority of teams and the people within them struggle with challenging conversations and conflict. Why aren't we embracing this as a tool to motivate, stimulate and support growth in ourselves and our people? From personal experience I would say the answer is because it is hard, and more often than not the anticipatory fear wins out over any possible positive outcome. So, what do we need as foundational elements to ensure we are taking full advantage of this wonderful opportunity?

In essence, people and teams need everything we've covered already in this book! A team whose culture is owned and driven from within will likely have clear boundaries and reference points on which to base hard conversations. If the people in those teams are consistently doing the work to increase their awareness both of themselves and others (see Chapter 7), conflict can be more skilfully embraced and navigated. Bringing up a challenge with a colleague is a hard thing to do and will make you feel uncomfortable, but if you come at it from a supportive angle it is the kind thing to do. Being able to sit with and explore points of friction is a mark of respect for your colleague and your team. If you are willing to embrace the vulnerability within your circles of trust, be curious about the conflict and remain open to the challenge, we can tap into so much magnificent growth potential.

The mindset

HELEN: For our team, embracing challenge and conflict had to be a very conscious process. According to our personality profiles we were naturally a very caring and nurturing team. Using positive encouragement to motivate change was a much more welcome method, though it didn't always achieve its intended result. The thought of being more explicit and the possibility of conflict didn't sit well with many team members, even if we recognised how important it was. Our various experiences had taught us that, unless we questioned the things we didn't agree with in an honest, open and timely fashion, it would lead to clandestine conversations and over time a lot of resentment. This is why we ended up with the behaviour statement 'We stamp out fires early' (see Chapter 3).

One of our teammates, Hannah Macleod, rightly kept banging this drum, and actually her openness and direct approach was something that helped us move beyond our discomfort to raise any issues we had. She would regularly remind us, 'We need more conflict,' and she was dead right. It was simple, and it effectively flipped our perspective on conflict from something we should avoid to something that would help us to be at our best. Another useful solution for meetings was to assign a 'devil's advocate'. Making it someone's job to think about the other side, to oppose what was being said just for the sake of it, freed up that person and also the whole group to think about things differently. These techniques were great ways for us to be open to challenging each other more. The more we welcomed differences of opinion, the more we realised that this didn't make us bad!

Even more significant was developing the skill of challenging our own mindset before delivering an opposing viewpoint. Framing hard conversations with the individual person in mind ensured that our messages were delivered from an angle of support and care, rather than dissatisfaction and irritation. By trying to humanise all our interactions we increased the chance that messages were accepted in the positive manner in which they were intended, and helped us to be more open to listening to understand instead of listening to respond. It's important to consider your mindset and how you view the intent of the people with whom you work. Your thoughts will affect your behaviours, your tone and the words you use. Trying to approach every potentially conflictual conversation with empathy and support will more likely incite powerful collaboration as opposed to destructive division.

Depending on what kind of a person you are, this might be really tough to work through. Many of us, myself included, have grown up believing that arguments are to be won or lost. However, as soon as you frame a conflict in this all-or-nothing way, no one actually 'wins'. One party might get their way, but at what cost? Without doubt I've missed out on building good relationships with teammates or coaches because of a conflict in our points of view. The problem wasn't so much that we were disagreeing but that we didn't try to understand where the other person was coming from. Starting these types of conversations are always hard. If you go into them ready to take responsibility for your part, with the goal of mutual understanding and agreement, you're more likely to get to a suitable outcome for all.

Making the most of the gift you've been given

KATE: All organisations have hierarchies. Of course they do; they reflect society and history. All teams within those organisations or companies also have their own levels or layers of power. These positions can be bestowed on people with titles and shiny corner offices, or they can be held as a result of charismatic personality traits that lead some to become informal team leaders. Breaking down these hierarchies is essential if you want your culture to be honestly and truly about everyone at every level. Of course, this is going to require sharing more, in every sense. Leaders must be prepared to be candid, vulnerable and honest more often. It's also necessary to share power, decision making and control. Only when challenge can be openly accepted across every layer of the organisation will you really be able to get the best from your team or organisation.

My initial reaction to challenge tends to be defensive, but as a leader of the team I quickly developed the sense that I needed to be more open to this type of feedback. The most difficult challenges were those that touched on my core values and that took the wind from my sails. However, after my gut reaction of denial and affront had subsided, I got curious about what had been said and considered what action I needed to take as a result of this nugget of information I had been gifted. Now, years later, I can say that every time I am challenged it is helpful.

One great example of a hierarchy being broken down and a leader dealing with challenge came for me in 2016 just a few months out from the Rio Olympic Games. I was towards the back end of my gym session doing my sets of chin-ups. I was one set in when one of the players came over in my rest break and said, 'Kate, I think you can put more weight on your belt – that looks too easy.' You can imagine how I reacted. Inside I was going through a whole gamut of emotions, and outwardly I think I must have showed that I'd had my feathers ruffled. In any case, nothing more was said between us. In every rest period for the rest of that session I thought about what she'd said and what I was doing. She was dead right and, to be honest, not just about my chin-ups!

I'd had a rough 18 months and I was just coming through that, allowing myself to simply drift to the end of my career, at least in some aspects of my training. That wasn't me, and, more importantly, it wasn't who we were as a team. My behaviour was totally against our culture, and that is what this player saw and what she was challenging me on. I was dismayed and proud all at once. I spoke to her after the session and said thank you because I knew that she had just been the best teammate I could have wished for at that moment. I asked her if she minded me sharing all of this with the team, and after she agreed I brought it up at the next player meeting. It was hard to replay the scenario and open myself up to the team; I had to be really brave. And my teammate choosing to challenge me in the authentic and respectful way she did made her brave, too.

Challenging people who are close to you is hard. I am still a work-in-progress in this respect. However, maybe it's age or experience but I am now more fearful of the consequences of *not* speaking up than of the challenge in and of itself. And this plays to a major learning point about challenge: try to tap into the motivation for the challenge and this should help you take the incentive. My teammate was tapping into our team behaviours that we had agreed on as part of our culture. It might be that the person's behaviour is challenging one of your organisation's moral or ethical values. You could find yourself in a position where you need to challenge someone to protect them, yourself or other people. It is these subtle moments of challenge where we as teams can really move forwards. I trust this woman implicitly and respect her unreservedly. She gave me a gift, and from that moment on I pushed myself harder again … and the rest is history. I feel that about every teammate that has ever demanded more or better from me. I know I wouldn't be the woman I am today without this challenge from them, and that is why the team and what it has given me will always be more important than any medal.

The problem with avoiding conflict

HELEN: It's easy to see why it would have taken a lot of courage for that player to go up to Kate to tell her that she thought she could be working harder. We've already spoken about the importance of vulnerability in order to build trust (see Chapter 6), and this ultimately sits at the heart of our willingness to challenge those around us, especially leaders. When trust doesn't exist, it becomes all too easy to avoid conflict at any cost. Instead, we resort to guarded conversations and empty discussions that don't get to the heart of the matter or address the elephant in the room.

This leads to a dangerous place for both individuals and the collective team. When we avoid conflict by not addressing the things that are causing frustration, we may keep the peace in that moment, but if we're not capable of letting it go, it has the propensity to eat us up from the inside out. From an individual perspective this isn't good for any of us. It's not good for our mental health, and it's not good for our performance. From a team perspective, there is no doubt that relationships will be affected negatively by not voicing our concerns. Without honest discussions and open disagreements, you will also end up with a group of people who won't be fully committed to the decisions that are made, even if there seems to be a consensus at the time.

Before 2009 we rarely had disagreements in any of our team meetings, and if we did, we rarely got down to the nitty-gritty of really thrashing things out before agreeing to a plan going forward. I think to some extent this is probably why the team visions we had prior to 2009 didn't have the impact they should have had. They were inspiring, ambitious goals, but maybe not everyone committed wholly because we didn't quite hear everyone's honest opinion. Without this certainty around a clear action plan, we lacked accountability to both ourselves and one another, and therefore we drifted into mediocrity.

Sometimes there are gigantic differences in opinion or huge frustrations being built up over time that need to be addressed. But there's also a fine line that the very best teams are able to navigate proficiently to tease out potential conflicts even before they come to them. When you get to that point it's such a motivating space to be in. I actually really enjoyed the debates we had during some of our team meetings in the latter years. I loved the fact that I got to hear the honest thoughts of my teammates, and actually it was a real privilege. One of those times was when we were developing our vision, values, and behaviours (VVB) for Rio. Going through this process meant our vision was very clear, as were our values and our behaviours. We all knew the plan, and we all knew, signed up to, and bought into how we were going to get there. This gave us guidelines to work within and allowed us to be held accountable and hold others to account in order to achieve the results we were after.

Boundaries and accountability

KATE: Interestingly, the person I had the most conflict with was myself! Like a lot of people, I was quite hard on myself, particularly in terms of my performance as an athlete. As a young player this self-criticism was pretty debilitating, but as I grew in confidence, I began to find a nice, honest balance. Always thinking I could do better was useful for me; it kept me motivated and hungry for more. As long as it didn't tip over into constant self-flagellation, self-challenge and a little bit of internal conflict were healthy for me. This internal check and challenge became second nature to me and helped me hold myself to account. I felt there was nothing more important I could do than to lead by example. Specifically, when we had agreed visions, values and behaviours I felt that above all else I needed to measure myself against that culture every day. I am responsible for myself, my thoughts and my actions, and it's here that I need to challenge myself before I can even think about challenging anyone else.

In our experience, in terms of holding yourself and others to account, boundaries can prove very helpful. As individuals and as a wider team we must have a clear understanding of expectations and boundaries so that we can know and understand where our limits are. In terms of your agreed team behaviours, what can be tolerated by the group and what would make the situation untenable? When we personally allow someone to cross our boundaries, or when we cross them ourselves, we can feel a huge amount of shame and resentment. In a team environment this can quickly build up and lead to some pretty toxic behaviours being shown as people hunker down into self-protection mode. Having a team understanding of tolerance levels also gives space for people to hold one another to account because there is a firm foundation from which to present challenge. These are courageous conversations and impactful interactions that can really drive team performance internally.

Boundaries also help provide some necessary guidance on how you hold one other to account as well. Without boundaries in this sense, it could very quickly become a finger-pointing blame game. In this game no one wins, as everyone can say whatever they want about whomever they want without thought, care or good intention. If this scenario was to play out in your team, how would you feel about being open, showing vulnerability and trusting your colleagues? If we want to create environments that are for everyone and that have trust, respect and belonging woven into their very fabric, then we must create team boundaries that guard against personal attacks and foster healthy conflict.

To be accountable is to be responsible, and when we had this in the team every player was fully bought in to driving themselves and each other. This is what success looks like; it is what makes your work fulfilling and facilitates growth for everyone. By embracing challenging conversations, you are effectively demonstrating that you care about this person, that you care about their growth. Plus, when you have grown a habit of giving and receiving feedback in this way, you are also boosting motivation, productivity, a sense of autonomy and ability to thrive.

When we create environments that encourage and welcome healthy airing of opinions and views, we are demonstrating our care for the team and ourselves. It requires courage to speak your mind and convey your emotions. Courage is also required when we receive this feedback and need to show gratitude for the gift that it is. Every time this happens we build trust, empathy and understanding of one another. When we welcome challenge, we welcome growth. This is not about arguing or pointing fingers; it is finding a way to communicate your opinion and listening to the opinions of others. If we can face our fears and sit with and share our emotions, we can unlock a deeper level of connectivity in our relationships. When we are connected as a team in this way; we are more resilient, we have a greater commitment to our goals, and we will flourish as people.

Avoiding conflict and challenge in a team setting is unhealthy both for you as an individual and your team. When we choose not to air our emotions and thoughts, they get stored away inside of us. Layer upon layer of stress, anger and frustration build up over time until one day, when we can take no more, it all spills out of us when we least expect it and least want it. This is, of course, draining and potentially very harmful for our mental and physical health. Well-being is something we must nurture and cherish in ourselves and in our teams, and embracing challenging conversations is certainly one way to do this. We will look at well-being and our need to give this time in more detail in the next chapter.

Team huddle

Conflict tends to arise through disagreements or perceived clashes around goals, values, interests or needs. The avoidance of addressing these moments of conflict does a disservice to all parties. When you face your fears and address challenging conversations in an empathetic and thoughtful way, you will aid growth and strengthen trust.

Questions to consider

- Are you a team that embraces positive conflict often? If not, what do you perceive to be the barriers to this in your team?
- Are you able to frame challenges so that they come from a place of support and care?
- What journey do you go on mentally and emotionally when you have been challenged or are experiencing conflict?
- Are the leaders role-modelling an openness to opposing ideas and differences of opinion?
- Are you best placed to make a challenge? Is there someone else with a stronger connection and a solid foundation of trust who might be better placed to have this conversation?

Key team tactics

- When you get a strong emotional reaction to a situation, give yourself some space to reflect and consider why you feel the way you do. See your thoughts and emotions with a compassionate lens and you will be more able to understand yourself and others.
- Before embarking on addressing a challenging situation, consider writing a short plan to help you navigate the conversation. Be clear with what you want to get out

of the conversation and be specific and clear with the points you want to make.

- Take frequent opportunities to air views and voice opinions in team environments to prevent the build-up of unaddressed moments of friction. Create your own rules of engagement in these meetings to help forge a safe space for open sharing.
- If your natural instinct is to avoid conflict, think about reframing the situation to help you take back some control. Challenge and conflict are not about arguing who is right and who is wrong. It is an opportunity to share how you're feeling and work to find solutions to make sure you don't feel like this again.
- If you are higher up the ladder in your organisational hierarchy, consider your position and how it might be impacting those you lead and the feedback they give you. Creating regular and informal opportunities to ask for honest opinions and points of view will benefit everybody in the long run.

9

Being well

We are reasonably well versed in the statistic that one in four of us experience mental health issues each year. As the world continues to move at a faster rate with escalating levels of uncertainty, there is an increasing need for each of us to find our own sense of stillness. We have both experienced difficulties with our mental health and have, at times, treated our well-being with flagrant disregard. In this chapter we will share our experiences; what we've learned, what helped, what hindered, what is key for us individually and what hopefully might help you.

As the saying goes, 'You can't pour from an empty cup', so we must all do what we can to care for ourselves. Our mind, body and soul are connected, and we must find space to attend to them all. This can feel overwhelming in an environment where we are constantly pushed for more output and better performances. Millions of working days and billions of pounds are lost to mental ill health each year. Leaders of organisations and teams must look beyond the figures and statistics and look to their people. Your people are your biggest asset; their biggest asset is their health. Look after their health, look after them – and everybody wins.

You're not alone

HELEN: In recent years I have been very open about my own struggles with my mental health, and the reason is simple. I can still remember how I felt when I opened Marcus Trescothick's autobiography, *Coming Back to Me*, and read the first page. For the first time I felt like I wasn't alone. I was relieved to know that it wasn't just me that was experiencing debilitating thoughts and feelings. Trescothick was a quality player, I loved watching him bat, so I was being reassured by someone at the top of their game. This could happen to anyone, and that was OK. Trescothick speaking up helped validate my feelings; he validated me. If I can do the same with just one other person by opening up here, it will have been worth it.

One of my biggest tells that something wasn't quite right was that I would just cry all the time, and I didn't know why. It definitely felt like something was happening inside of me, but I had no clue what it was and absolutely no idea how to make it stop. I know a lot of people who've suffered with depression talk about being in a dark place, and that was exactly the same for me. In the middle of a crying fit I would desperately say to myself, 'I don't know what to do', over and over again. In those moments I knew I needed help, but I didn't know why, I didn't know what I needed help for, and I hadn't the foggiest idea of how to get it.

A big turning point and a moment of comfort was when I finally shared how I was feeling. I didn't plan it; I was seeing our team doctor about something else and when he asked me how I was it all came out. The act of opening up was hard and important, but more significant than that was the fact he gave it a name. When he said the word 'depression', instead of feeling fearful, I felt relief. This was a *thing*. This meant there was something I could do about it. This gave me the ability to take back some sort of control.

At my lowest point, I didn't know why I felt like I did, and even a few years later I couldn't understand it. I thought things in my life were going reasonably well. Looking back now I can see that I'd undergone some quite big changes in my life: relationships, living abroad for the first time, and playing in a team with very high expectations in a place where I didn't speak the language. I thought I was dealing with these things OK, but maybe I wasn't. When I was younger, I never really shared what was going on inside me. I didn't like to talk about my feelings; it always felt awkward. I've attributed some of that to feeling like I had to hide a massive part of me, so not being quite sure of my sexuality and who I was, was part of the problem I think. Storing away my emotions meant they slowly and silently built up over time, without my being able to process any of them along the way – I do wonder if it was a case of life finally catching up with me. I now understand how important it is to have an outlet for whatever is going on inside you.

If you're thinking, 'What's my private life got to do with work or my team?', my answer is 'Everything!' If it's not you who's struggling right now, there will more than likely be people in your team who are and they will benefit from your support. The more we share our own personal experiences, the easier it becomes to empathise from a place of understanding. Although it took for me to be at my lowest point to get the support I needed, it doesn't have to be that way. There is so much we can all do as individuals and as employers to ensure that we and our people are as well as can be, and it starts with talking about mental health.

We all have mental health

HELEN: With every passing year 'mental' and 'health' are two words that are being said together more and more. Thinking back just a few years to when we won gold in 2016, we were nowhere near where we are now; although there is still a long way to go, within sport and as a society we are beginning to understand that our mental health is a concern for each and every one of us and with it there is a growing acceptance that it is something that can be protected and nurtured. With most of us spending around a third of our lives at work, it's safe to say your job can have a huge impact on your quality of life. Companies and organisations have to acknowledge their responsibility and the part they must play in maximising the health of their employees. The target shouldn't simply be the absence of physical or mental illness; being well needs to imply a sense of flourishing and enjoying what you do. Those that bloom have a better chance of bringing their best to whatever it is they're doing; an added bonus to having a thriving workforce will always be an uprise in performance.

From my own experience and from meeting countless others with similar stories, I have come to realise that, as with physical health, we all have mental health and we all sit on a spectrum from being well to unwell, sliding up and down the scale depending on what life decides to throw at us. Those who roll their eyes and accuse people of jumping on the mental health 'bandwagon' are simply missing the point. We all have mental health – there, I said it again! The more we appreciate that the better chance we all have of being as well as we can be, regardless of where we sit on the spectrum. That has to be our aim.

Talk it up and help break the taboo

HELEN: I can probably count on one hand the number of times mental health was mentioned during our playing careers. As we've already shared, during the latter years there was lots of support in place in various forms, and the culture we created implied a degree of understanding, but to actually hear those specific words was very rare. This is an important distinction to make. There is a strong and deep-rooted stigma attached to the phrase 'mental health'. Chances are, on hearing it yourself, your brain conjured up illnesses such as depression or anxiety; I know mine used to. We instinctively go to the dark end of the spectrum, where we've been convinced over decades or even centuries that poor mental health signifies weakness, and should be something to be ashamed of.

Certainly, my number one fear about opening up was that I might be seen differently or as weak. I was the vice-captain of the team, and I was worried that people would think I couldn't cope with the demands of elite sport or the extra responsibility leadership places on you. I was scared these things would be taken away from me. When we bring mental health into our conversations, it takes away that drama! The only way to break this stigma is to bring it out into the light. To talk about it, how it really exists in the lives of real people, with real lives and real problems.

KATE: We all have a significant role to play with this, particularly in our place of work and especially if we are a leader. In my work as a business coach, I have spoken to a large number of people in leadership roles and I can see that Helen's fear is very common. Many of them still hold the belief that as a leader they shouldn't show a vulnerability such as a mental health problem because it will make them appear weak. What we are afraid of is being labelled; I know I'm the same. Labels are hard to shift as they are born out of years of history and storytelling. So, in any organisational context the best and most important thing you can do as a leader is to break down the labels, the stereotypes and the history.

My relationships with my teammates changed for the better after I had shared my mental health struggles with them. I found that in return they were more able to talk and share their own experiences with me. This took a lot of courage from them and me and could only have been done in the safe space we created and after trust was well established, as we have discussed throughout the book. By role-modelling that it was OK not to be OK, we allowed others to open up to ask themselves if they were OK. When leaders authentically talk about and share their personal mental health journey, it has a huge impact on those they lead. It simply says: this is usual, this is OK and I'm here with you at an empathetic level. It breaks down the stigma and strips away the labels.

We only really scratched the surface of talking about mental health towards the very end of my career. But it could not have been more timely for me. I have been in many teams over the years where my teammates would have benefited enormously from having the support and the opportunity to share so openly. It was devastating to see my teammates so clearly going through challenging times and my not having the knowledge or understanding to know what to do to help them. You may have experienced this yourself with people in your own life.

Nowadays, there is much more understanding, help and support out there for us all, when we are ready to embrace it. We must give this the time and care it deserves, for ourselves, for the people around us, for everyone. When conversations around mental health become a regular occurrence, it creates a solid foundation from which to promote well-being across the whole team.

Promoting positive mental health

HELEN: As individuals, and as employers, we must make time for recovery. It's well known that 'rest' days from hard training are critical for reaching peak physical fitness, and the same is true for our mental well-being. Stressors in the form of challenges are unavoidable within life, and if we are to grow and learn, they're also good for us. But importantly, too, our brains need time to recover from that stress. The build-up of continual stress without an outlet to recover increases the potential for burnout or developing a mental illness, and in a world where we are constantly 'available' through our electronic devices this is becoming more prevalent than ever before. Most of us are pretty well practised at recovering naturally by doing things such as connecting with friends and family, playing recreational sports or indulging in the arts and cultural experiences; and sleep, exercise and nutrition, too, of course, are the bedrock to good mental health. I eventually found mindfulness to be my lifesaver (along with therapy, medication and golf), as it taught me not to judge my thoughts and feelings. I needed to be kinder to myself. When we don't give ourselves the time to enjoy these aspects of our lives, or when these things are taken away from us, as they were during the COVID-19 pandemic, the stress builds up over time and the cup can overflow.

When the squad was discussing what our full-time training programme should look like in the build-up to the London Olympics, we talked about the importance of recovery in every aspect – between training sessions, throughout the week, over a month's period and even the whole year ahead. What lay ahead was relatively unknown, but there was a feeling that what we were about to embark on was going to take us farther out of our comfort zones than ever before, physically, of course, but also mentally and emotionally. To enable our recovery, we included a week every month that had no hockey training at all. For one week out of four we had a bit more control over where we trained and with whom. We still had a very comprehensive and hard physical programme to follow, but we could do this wherever we wanted. This week gave respite for our bodies, our brains and from each other, with the overall aim of getting us ready to 'go again' in the next three-week effort. Arriving at this decision took a bit of guesswork, but once the programme started it became clear that three weeks on the bounce was ideal. On the odd occasion when we had to do four weeks in a row, we all knew about it from the tetchy atmosphere!

When you're striving to achieve, it's so easy to think that you need to fill the time, do more and work harder. I think that's what a lot of people from outside of our bubble thought we were doing. It made me chuckle when I heard rumours that the whole squad were living together at our training base, training together, eating together, basically in each other's pockets 24/7.

No wonder we were criticised! Some countries even copied what they thought we were doing, but because they didn't know the truth, they left out the most important bit – recovery. How to achieve optimum performance in sport and work – and life for that matter – has changed: it's not about doing more, it's about being smart.

There were still many improvements we could have made in this area. You could ask, for example, why we needed a break after three weeks' training – surely there must have been something wrong with the overall balance during the training weeks? And you'd be right to question that. Even if you think you've got this area covered, keep asking yourself: what more can we do? Whatever form it takes, we all need to give time to giving back to ourselves. Rest and recovery are so incredibly important for our mental health as well as our performance. No one can go full steam ahead all of the time, and giving time for employees to rest and recover is imperative. Being able to switch off phones, with no pressure to answer emails when not at work, goes a long way in helping people thrive and not just survive.

KATE: When we could train where we wanted in our fourth week it also gave us choice and freedom to do what was right for us in that moment. In the same way, companies can provide flexible working hours and even flexibility of work location to give their employees that same sense of control. It is this small sense of self-management that can be so helpful in replenishing energy stores. When employers provide this flexibility it also says that we care about you as a whole person. It says we understand that you might have caring responsibilities of children or elderly relatives. It says that we value not only what you do here with us but also the other aspects of your lives.

There were times, as an athlete, when I felt I was being treated as a body that was providing data rather than a living breathing human being. Over the course of my playing career, I have also been encouraged to take all and every bit of feedback like a robot and remove all emotion from the exchange. Because I am someone who feels deeply and whose emotions are important to how I exist in the world, this wasn't just unhelpful but potentially hugely damaging. Through my experiences of having been treated this way by leaders I feel very passionately that we must all do better to value the whole person and all that they are. We are so much more than the sum of our output or contribution to profits. How we view and value the people in our care says a lot about the leadership and the organisation. When we lose sight of the people and only see figures and data we are missing out on so much worth and potential.

Connecting with people and a purpose

KATE: Connection is so important at all times but especially when we are struggling with our mental health, low mood or low energy. It was the loss of connectivity that was mourned by most employees I spoke to during the first year of the COVID-19 global pandemic, as many millions of people were forced to work from home. This connectivity and kinship are found in the small everyday moments in a team environment. For me, as an athlete, it was the conversations with teammates as we sat in the dugout before training commenced, the eye contact of a shared moment that would set you both off laughing, a quick chat as we walked to our cars at the end of the day. These small windows of time when you inhabit each other's worlds for a few minutes are so precious. And, like most special things, we don't fully appreciate what we have until it has gone. While we can't always control how we connect, we can find ways to make it work to ensure we maintain those important bonds through both good and challenging times.

As the importance of caring for our mental health has crept up the priority list, many organisations have started to provide lots of great opportunities for employees to connect with others both inside and outside the company. Almost all companies now have various internal networks that you can join as allies or members. As Helen mentioned above, recovery is key, but this doesn't always mean doing nothing – doing *something different* is sometimes the respite we need. I've seen companies encourage their employees to volunteer for a day and still be paid. Helping others can benefit our own mental health, and simple acts of kindness can reduce stress as well as improve mood, self-esteem and happiness.

Our team's vision for Rio partially looked beyond the group itself and instead honed in on what impact we could have on society more broadly. What it meant to 'Be the difference, create history and inspire the future' looked a little different to everyone depending on where their passions lay. For Helen and I, one of our big passions is disability sports: we gave, and continue to give, our time and energy to supporting the charity Access Sport which helps give disadvantaged and disabled people the opportunity to play sport. In particular, we support its disability hockey programme called Flyerz. I can honestly say that the days we've spent with Flyerz teams and other disability hockey teams have been some of my best days – they remind me of why I love our sport, hockey, and the joy of the players is contagious.

Connectedness to other people can help with our mental health, but, as you can see, the same is true of connectedness to a purpose. It is widely accepted that when we have a strong purpose and are actively engaged in the pursuit of that purpose, we are more likely to have positive mental health. Certainly, in the build-up to London 2012 and then Rio 2016, we had a strong sense of team and individual purpose and as a result, on the whole, I felt energised. When I felt like I'd lost my sense of purpose in 2014, and again when I retired from hockey in 2016, I felt adrift and rudderless. In both instances my mental wellness became increasingly troubling for me. I didn't realise this necessarily at the time; I just felt very low more often than not. What I learned going through these challenging periods was that my sense of self and my purpose is inextricably linked to my mental health. My circumstances may change, things will happen that are out of my control, but if I hold on to who I am and where I am going, I will be OK.

It's OK to not be OK, but help needs to be at hand

KATE: Of course, for many people, no matter how well their whole self is cared for and nourished, they will still suffer with a mental illness. And it doesn't discriminate. Mental illness doesn't care what job you do, how much money you've got or where you live, although our individual circumstances can absolutely have an impact on our access to treatment and opportunity to tend to our mental ill health in the most effective way. I feel so very fortunate and lucky to have experienced mental health difficulties at a time when there was provision and support available. I know that the socio-economic privileges provided by my upbringing and my career in sport gave me the privilege of specialist treatment when I needed it most. The cost of private mental health support prices a great deal of the population out, and the state-funded sector is buckling under the weight of a growing need.

We only started having formal links with specialist mental health providers in my final years of playing. Through our private medical insurance, we could gain access to The Priory – an important private provider of mental health facilities in the UK – for a number of sessions, and this initial foot in the door was a saving grace for many. It most certainly came to my rescue at a time when I felt entirely lost. In 2014, I found that I had no ability to regulate or even comprehend my emotional state. I was erratic and volatile. I was sad and inconsolable. Like Helen, I went to see our doctor about an ankle injury I had sustained and I ended up falling to pieces in a big messy outburst. He went through some questions and assured me that support was there for me if I wanted it. I remember feeling some relief just knowing that there was somewhere I could go to get help. I attended The Priory as an outpatient, on a weekly basis at first but then, over time, at longer intervals. It was a lifeline, and I clung on to it dearly. Each session was exhausting and emotionally draining. Some weeks I felt like I was going backwards, but over the period of about 15 months or so I felt like I was coming back to myself. Having that outside support and fresh perspective on life proved invaluable to me.

It is vital that all places of work provide the opportunity to access specialist support to all those who may need it. Having visible points of reference on internal online servers and in workplaces will mean that people are certainly more likely to reach out. Having leaders that are able to share their experiences of accessing this support will again help break down some of the barriers to getting help. Helen and I went on a mental health first aid course and learned an incredible amount, and this is relevant to all organisations and the people within them. Having mental health first aiders in your place of work could make all the difference for someone who is experiencing any form of mental ill health. When support becomes more readily available and mental health becomes more visible, it becomes less of a taboo subject. In the end we all need support in our lives; it is a team game after all. Building our support networks to help us when we're OK and when we're not OK is the greatest form of teamwork there is.

Is this how I want to be feeling?

HELEN: In writing this chapter one thing that has become quite clear to us is how Kate and I both compromised our own mental health for hockey. I do think there is more that needs to be done within sport so others don't end up doing the same, though personally I don't blame anyone for that (that said, I know other athletes would disagree); I don't think anyone would have been able to change my single-mindedness and how I went about my business. But is there a line to be drawn?

Just two weeks after Rio, Kate and I were walking along the Thames in Windsor and I said, 'What was the point of any of that?' My question was fuelled by me reminiscing about the 18 years we'd both given to our national team and now thinking, 'Well, here we are back home. What now?' It was said somewhat tongue in cheek and I was probably suffering from post-tournament blues, but there was some truth in it: we had done what we, and the team, had wanted – we'd created history – but where did that leave us now? My body was literally in tatters. I had pain in my ankle, my hamstring, my hips, my back, my knees and my big toe! And my brain hurt. A lot. By the end, the final few years felt like some kind of weird paradox. Mentally, I was clinging on for dear life, struggling to get through each day. A decade and a half of fighting had taken its toll. I was weighed down by so much of the past and the constant challenge to be better that now my emotions were constantly on the edge. But it was exactly that challenge that made me feel so alive mentally. It was a good challenge. I was growing. I was developing. I was listening and engaging in new ways all the time. The contradiction was real. I struggled to get my head round feeling broken but flourishing at the same time! I needed to stop and yet I wanted to keep playing for ever.

What made this paradox more intriguing was the way in which I thought about how success 'should be' had changed. The old me believed that success, especially in sport, needed to be hard. My own experience of hardship had made me think that nothing does or should come easy. You have to suffer before tasting glory. Then the new part of me, probably through suffering too much, knew that it didn't have to be this way. What's the point in achieving your dream if you're left broken at the end of it? The sentiment of 'Life's hard, get on with it' doesn't quite ring true anymore. Yes, life *is* hard. When we experience things like heartbreak, anxiety, sadness or failure, it's hard. And yes, we all have to get on and continue one way or another, but what's changed is that we no longer have to endure it alone and in silence. No longer should it be a mark of strength to be able to get through a day's work without anyone noticing that you're struggling through one of life's difficulties.

KATE: Like Helen, I pushed myself far beyond my limits on a regular basis; it has come to be expected of all elite athletes. I sometimes asked far too much of myself mentally and emotionally, though. This impacted me in ways I am only now fully coming to terms with years after I have retired. I also know that what I asked of myself I also asked of my teammates and even staff around me. I fear that I impacted them in the same way. I don't think I would want to remove all that pushing for excellence and constant improvement. To be the very best at something, I believe, is always going to be a demanding journey. However, knowing what I know now, about my mental health and that of the people around me, I would certainly approach situations in a different way and with alternative methods. If well-being had been in my consciousness, I would have wanted the same push for excellence but with a disclaimer that the mental health of everyone must come first. Above all else, no prize is worth risking how well we are.

We may never be able to take full control of our mental wellness, but what we can do is bring awareness to it and tend to its needs. By listening to and caring for ourselves in this way we give ourselves the best opportunity to thrive. If we are able to tap into purpose, connect with people, and rest when we need to, we can support our well-being with true autonomy by controlling what we can. The more we talk about and share our personal experiences, the more readily stigma and labels are broken down, allowing us to live our truest life. We are not alone. You are not alone.

Really what it comes down to is being kind. To be kind is to be friendly, generous and considerate. Kindness starts from a place of understanding that we all struggle from time to time. It is the gift we can all afford to give more of, starting with ourselves. This key human quality is needed now more than ever in a world that is increasingly polarised and divided. When we treat ourselves with compassion we will flourish, in viewing others through the same lens we see the beauty and complexity in our difference and they too get to be their best selves. In the next chapter we will look at diversity and how being treated with respect and care and treating others in the same way can be our greatest strength.

Team huddle

We all have mental health, and it can have a huge impact on your daily life, your relationships and your physical health. Looking out for and looking after your own mental health is critical in a world that is increasingly volatile and uncertain. The more you understand your own mental health, the more able you will be to help others with theirs. Creating safe spaces that support people talking about mental health will help destigmatise mental ill health. Ending the taboo will enable more people to seek the specialist help and support needed to live a fulfilling and whole life.

Questions to consider

- How do you feel about your current mental and physical state?
- What do you need in your life to help you feel good about your mental health and well-being?
- What are the potential barriers to you feeling well, both mentally and physically?
- Where do you feel you have a sense of control and purpose in your life?
- What activities replenish your energy?
- Where can you show yourself more kindness? Where can you show others more kindness?

Key team tactics

- In all of the networks and teams in which you reside, spend time talking and sharing personal experiences of mental and physical well-being. Practise good listening: listen to understand and not necessarily to respond. Keep kindness at the front and centre of every conversation.
- Once you've identified what activities replenish your energy, make time for them. Bring them into your daily,

weekly and monthly routines by actively putting them in your diary.

- Engage with books, podcasts or articles that share personal stories of mental health and well-being. Consider what resonates and reflect on where this has shown up in your life or of those around you. Connecting with people in this way helps us understand that we are not alone and that there is help and support when we need it.

- Sharing your personal well-being tools with those you trust will create immediate support networks and a place of connection and understanding. Your trusted inner circle can also provide sensitive nudges for you when perhaps you need them most.

IO

Embracing difference

As humans we are so incredibly different from one another. A team's inability to embrace this difference as a key strength can lead to toxic culture
and environments. When we feel we are valued fully for our exceptional
contribution, we are more likely to feel engaged, motivated and safe to
push ourselves beyond the limits. If there is equity of opportunity across
a diverse population, we can all feel a greater sense of belonging and purpose. And if you are the type of person or team that is purely motivated
by results and performance, then you'll be pleased to know that embracing difference with openness and transparency will also have a huge
impact on your ultimate success. When we leveraged on the differences
we had, and used it as a powerful force, we saw a huge shift in our outcome and potential growth. Taking time to fully understand each of our
unique qualities also provided us with an important opportunity to form
bonds of trust and respect, which sit at the heart of every high-performing team. When everyone is viewed as an integral part of the circle as
opposed to a peripheral 'other' forced to the margins, then we are living
up to our potential as people and teams.

The strength of our team was the entire squad of people. Not just
the 16 you saw standing on the top of the podium with gold medals
around our necks, but the whole team of 31 players and the ten members
of our management team. When the 31 players understood what each
of us could bring individually and at the same time make sure that the
environment was the best for all, we found our esprit de corps. There was
a sense of togetherness, solidarity and pride that elevated us to levels far
beyond what others thought were possible. The opportunity for a sport
like hockey – and many organisations – is the vast untapped potential of
currently marginalised people. If we were able to build the culture that we

did with very little diverse thought, life experience and background, just imagine what could be accomplished when we work assiduously to create open, transparent and equitable opportunity for everyone.

Stand for something or stand for nothing

KATE: As a young person I definitely felt the pressure to 'fit in'. I'm not sure if I really wanted to be in the inner circle or the 'in crowd' or whether I was just afraid of what it meant to be on the outside of those circles and groups. Conformity was also something I experienced as a young hockey player. I understood that there was a mould that I needed to shoehorn myself into in order to progress. Fortunately for me, being white, cis-gendered, middle class and able-bodied, I could do that with relative ease. Reflecting back I can see the appeal for those in positions of authority to move towards selecting players who were 'known' quantities. Those coaches were judged on their results, which needed to be delivered with very little preparation or development time. I can also see that when coaches and selectors behaved in this way it was ultimately wrong, harmful and prejudiced. Systemic and systematic discrimination shows itself in sport as it does in business and all other areas of society, and there are no reasons or excuses big enough to make any of this right. How often have you or I considered who the systems we all circulate in are designed by and for? Have we ever given a moment's thought to the people who the systems are designed without?

We have never had much diversity in terms of race or social class playing international hockey in the UK. It certainly felt like the talent pathway was a conveyor belt of people more or less like me. The robotic churning out of players that look the same, sound the same and play the same is still a big cause for concern. There have been a handful of players who have broken the mould over the years in some way and made it, despite the odds being stacked against them. Long before terms like 'microaggressions' and 'stereotypical tropes' were fully in our consciousness, there were people, human beings, who were and continue to deal with this, and worse, every day. Within the almost exclusively white teams that I have played in, there were some players with a difference in identity, perspective, language and point of view and this was not always fully welcomed. I remember one player who didn't conform to what a stereotypical white middle-class woman should look and sound like. She stood up in a meeting room one day as a relatively new player to feed back from her group's discussion and after a few words was rudely cut off by the coach. He wanted her to start again and to speak 'properly'. Aside from the absolute sense of shame she so clearly felt, there was also a sense of complete confusion. She was speaking English – what was it about how she was speaking that made it 'improper' and how could she address that in the midst of the meeting? We rallied around her privately but failed to challenge those in power. It was a lesson for me that how we treat people who are different from ourselves says a lot more about us than it does about them. Saying nothing in support of those being discriminated against makes me complicit.

Thinking differently

KATE: Interestingly, and perhaps unsurprisingly, the question I get asked a great deal when I am presenting keynotes to businesses is 'How do you deal with the mavericks?' I sometimes ask them to clarify what they mean by 'maverick', and generally the answer I get is that it is someone who is pushing the team's cultural boundaries, a person who thinks differently and has a different perspective from others. I respond with honesty that my thoughts around this have changed over my career. In the beginning I felt I needed to uphold the leadership and keep people on the same page, make sure no one strayed outside the boundaries or strayed off line. I felt that my role as a captain was to uphold the views of the coach and lead with that in mind. Over time I realised that I was silencing people, holding back on my own views, and, in doing so, harming our potential as a team.

In attempting to keep the peace and avoid friction, we aid the suppression of challenge and growth. In actual fact, the very thing I wanted to avoid was actually the very thing we most needed. We need difference; we need to be inclusive of different thinkers and different perspectives. If we do not embrace diversity of thought, we are missing the greatest opportunity to make better decisions and choices as a team. Only by giving everybody the platform to speak up can we ever robustly challenge traditional and embedded views. Friction and discomfort must be chosen over comfort and ease if we truly want to reach our potential as teams and as people.

From my experience, there is a very critical line in the sand here for people that push the boundaries in a team environment, and that line is based around energy. If a team member is consistently taking more energy than they are giving back to the team, then this signifies the need for a significant intervention. Sometimes it just isn't the right fit, and while that is a difficult reality to accept, there comes a time when the best interests of the team must come first.

Be curious – see and embrace all our differences,
including your own

HELEN: When our team culture was at its very best, reaching our potential as people both individually and as a collective was at the centre, and it took all of our voices to understand what that meant for every single one of us. In order to create opportunities for each of us to thrive and flourish we first needed to work hard to establish what our individual and collective best looked like. Being supported to work through the exercises we discussed in the chapters on awareness and vulnerability helped us develop that necessary sense of self. We worked hard on ourselves and the acceptance of ourselves and indeed each other; only once we had wholly accepted ourselves could we truly belong anywhere. Another powerful tool we utilised in both the London and Rio Olympic cycles was the use of personality profiling. When used well they are hugely positive tools that can open up reflective thought and stimulate conversation in teams. When they are misused, they can prove to be restrictive and too definitive in their conclusions. Thankfully, our psychologists worked exceptionally hard so that we collectively struck the right balance.

Once again, as with everything we've said throughout this book, it wasn't enough to simply complete the personality questionnaire, be given our results and expect the understanding of ourselves and each other to somehow seep into our consciousness. This took a huge amount of effort, time and hard work, as well as challenging many of our personal perceptions, including my own. I now know that how we all see and understand the world around us is shaped by who we are, how we interact and how it intersects with the systems and structures on which our society and cultures are built. When my personality is mixed together with any and all of my lived experiences such as my gender, my sexuality, my upbringing, my race, the people around me, my education, my job, my opportunity, it creates me and determines how and why I behave in the way I do. All these blended elements come together to conceive a unique individual, as is the case for us all. We are all one of a kind. Not right or wrong, not better or worse, just different.

Our personality profiles helped us understand our own and each other's natural styles, our strengths, the value we all brought to the team and how we like to communicate and be communicated with. Honest dialogue helped us realise that too many of us weren't feeling empowered enough to bring our instinctive energies, and this meant we were missing out on too much leadership potential. We all had our insecurities. Those who were direct and assertive feared being labelled aggressive, contentious or unkind. The social energy givers thought they were too often seen as frivolous and not serious enough. Those who valued reasoning and logic were worried about seeming overly critical and boring. And those whose energy came from care and consideration felt the pressure of a perceived lack of urgency. The majority of these feelings purely came from assumptions inside the head of the individual feeling them. In most cases there was nothing but our own imaginations to back these assumptions up. The very nature of having these conversations was therefore enough to liberate our minds. We recognised that we needed the whole array of personality traits – the aggression, the care, the fun, the critical thinking – and, importantly, it was helpful to know who, more often than not, would bring each element. But we also acknowledged that we should not be constrained by our preferences, as every one of us has the ability to access all these traits. Knowing this gave us permission to bring all of ourselves and deliver a valuable role for the team.

Our personality profiles became a vehicle for curiosity within all of our relationships. The more curious you are to where colleagues are coming from, the more you ask questions and the more you assume you can learn from everyone, the more you are freed from judgement – and not just of others but also of yourself. Acknowledging our differences makes it OK to have a clash of personalities. We won't all get on with everyone in life, and that's not good or bad; it just is, and that's OK. Accepting this helps you to overlook the things you may dislike, and learn how to work well with one another when it's necessary for the sake of the team.

Being women

KATE: We became adept at performing to a high level alongside people who thought and functioned differently from ourselves. As I've mentioned at the beginning of the chapter, though, on the whole, as a group we weren't different enough and so it could be assumed that all of this came relatively easy to us. One similarity that would always bind us together was our gender. We all identified as women. Our womanhood was our connection. In many ways I think how much more powerful our collective voice would have been if we had thought about ourselves in this way more often. We were, and are, all privileged – that is beyond doubt. For the vast majority of people in our team, being white and our lack of a physical disability did not affect our ability to thrive. In this way we were in the powerful majority. However, we did find ourselves often on the other side of the power divide when it came to our gender. Because in sport, as it is in almost all other areas of society, women are considered lesser than the men.

Yes, even hockey, a sport that you might consider a predominantly female sport, suffers from sexism all the way through from top to bottom. We often look to Olympic and Paralympic sports as bastions of gender equality in the modern era. You need only scratch the surface of that shiny veneer, though, to reveal the bare-faced reality. While the women's and men's programmes were, to my knowledge, always funded by UK Sport based on performance and our access to coaches and national training facilities was equal, this is probably where gender equality started and ended. Recently, I discovered that a personal sponsor offered one of my male counterparts four times the money I had managed to negotiate for myself. The reason for the discrepancy was put down to the fact that he had more opportunities to show off the sponsor in the European Hockey League and the Hockey India League. As there wasn't and still isn't an equivalent of these events for women, I couldn't compete. I would never be able to realise my financial sponsorship value because the game was rigged against me and all other women. But value is about a lot more than money, and it is the daily layering of micro-aggressions that are the hardest thing to contend with. Typically, microaggressions are offensive comments or actions directed at a member of a marginalised group, especially a racial minority. I've used it in this instance to reference the numerous examples of misogyny I and we experienced as female athletes.

The thing with microaggressions is that on their own they can seem meaningless and petty, particularly to someone who either isn't experiencing them or isn't aware that they are. Not having kit that fits you because – let's face it – unisex means small man size was considered the norm at the Olympic level and was something we just 'had to get on with'. Yes, we were grateful for any kit at all. Yes, we are the privileged few. But our gratefulness over the years has been weaponised and used against us as women. Through our supposed need to be grateful and humble it has allowed the status quo to remain intact without any question or challenge to what is right. We have been kicked off the main hockey pitch because the men needed to train that night, even though it was the women's slot. We have not had a home changing room assigned to us by our own club, while the men's first team have a huge room for them and them alone. Aside from a couple of seasons in the Netherlands, we have paid to play for our club our whole lives, whereas the vast majority of male internationals, and even some men who have never played for their country, have never paid and in actual fact have been reimbursed financially in some way for their efforts. We have been treated as lesser because of our gender our whole lives, and this has not only reinforced the strength of those in power but chipped away at our own sense of worth and power.

Our words have power

HELEN: Another area of our lives where we've felt lesser is because of our sexuality. As with the examples Kate has given above, there are very similar ones when you identify as LGBTQ+. Heteronormativity is so ingrained in the fabric of our society it dominates the way we communicate with one another to the point where our biases are so inherent we don't even realise when we think or voice them. I'm even including myself in that because I, like everyone else, was brought up to believe that intimate relationships should be between a woman and a man. We must be mindful of our words to acknowledge our differences. Saying 'partner' instead of 'husband' or 'wife' might seem like nothing to you, but to me it demonstrates that you value me enough to not make assumptions or judgements about who I might be. Language is incredibly powerful and it can include or exclude; Kate and I were asked by a journalist whether we were 'trying to make a statement' by double-barrelling our surnames. This made us feel like we didn't have the same right to share a name like the majority of straight couples choose to do. Heterosexual sporting couples in the public eye are celebrated even before they get engaged, let alone married, but here Kate and I were being 'othered'. That journalist devalued our relationship and by doing so devalued us as human beings.

It wasn't until I was challenged on my language that I started to think about how my words could be hurtful to others. As a teenager, and without giving the meaning of it a moment's thought, I started using the derogatory phrase 'That's so gay'. I was just mindlessly repeating what was being said around me (this was way before I had come out myself). I was new into the senior GB team and said it at dinner one evening, and a teammate across the table simply said, 'Don't say that. I find it offensive.' Her straight face showed no trace of a joke, and I instantly realised she was deadly serious. I quickly figured it out and sheepishly apologised – I never said it again and called out anyone that did.

The ignorance of youth, of course, is no excuse, and I was grateful to my teammate for her no-nonsense approach in pointing mine out to me. As Maya Angelou said, 'Do the best you can until you know better. Then when you know better, do better.' Twenty years on and I'm saddened to hear that phrase still being used. With young people I can kind of get it; that was me back in the day, which is why conversation, education and the use of stories are powerful tools we must adopt – they help to open our hearts and minds to our differences and increase understanding of the impact of our words. But when a coach of ours, a grown man said it, not once, but twice, even after I called him out the first time, I was utterly dismayed. Saying you didn't mean it like that, or pointing out you have a gay friend, doesn't justify comments like these, ever. Our words and actions hold weight, and they can hurt people.

The experience of being a gay person in sport was definitely made more positive by being female. I am grateful to have grown up and lived in an environment that, in general, was open to all sexualities. There are obviously people who think that we are wrong for living our lives, but we have come through relatively unscathed. Even when Kate and I as a couple became higher profile through the success of our team, between us we have received only a handful of hateful remarks. We don't go looking for it, mind you; I will actively avoid specific Twitter feeds where I know negative comments are more prevalent. But to be a gay man in sport is a different story altogether, and contemplating the possibility of out gay or bisexual male professional footballers in particular is often held up as the marker for real progress. This weighty burden of responsibility does not lie with individual male footballers. This is the responsibility of us all: to create a society and places of work where everybody belongs. Only when we positively start to break down the stereotypes, norms and expectations for all people will we ever progress in sport, business and all areas of society.

KATE: One such negative stereotype we encountered, particularly from people outside of our team bubble, was around our relationship within the team. Rarely have people asked how wonderful it must have been or what were the positives of working together. We are often asked how we coped as a couple and more so how the team coped with the reality of two of the team being in a relationship. It worked for us, and we think it worked for the team because we wanted it to work and we worked hard to find a way that was best for everyone. Helen and I were very clear with our professional and personal boundaries from the offset. We had some uncomfortable conversations with our coaches and the team that were hugely important to ensure that there was openness and honesty about our intentions and how we all wanted everything to work. It helped that we were all aligned around our culture and we all wanted what was best for the team. I felt that in just having this level of conversation with the people we were interacting with on a daily basis normalised something that wasn't perhaps currently seen as normal.

We are so grateful that players and staff were open-minded. I'm not sure everyone agreed or understood our relationship, but I did feel that there was a commitment from everyone to be professional and respectful. For a team to fully embrace all forms of diversity and all of our individual life experiences, it must start with space to talk, time to be heard and a lot of listening with care. If our coaches and teammates had shut down our need to be our whole selves, then we would have suffered and ultimately, to a certain extent, so would the team. We must all, especially those in the powerful majority, ask ourselves constantly who are we shutting down, who are we silencing and who are we pushing even farther to the margins. I remain a work in progress on this and will for the rest of my life. I know that really phenomenal teams are inclusive of diversity and prosper because together we can be so much stronger. The human race is the team we're all on, we all have value, we all have worth, we all have vital roles to play, and only when we allow everyone to play those roles can we reach our fullest potential.

It's not good enough to claim ignorance anymore: to be inactive against any form of discrimination or oppression is as bad as the acts themselves. We must be the change we wish to see; we owe it to the memories of those gone before us, to the next and future generations, and to humanity in this moment today. By choosing to be that change and be that role model for a better tomorrow and today we continue to build momentum in the movement. The amount of knowledge that surrounds us is plentiful: there are books, articles, podcasts, TV shows, radio talk shows, a plethora of social media content ... The list is endless. The information is there to be found if you really want it — it's time to do the work. What is it like to walk in the shoes of someone that doesn't fit the constructed norms that were created by and for the same group of people? We all need to listen, to understand, to empathise, but we also need to be active in breaking down the barriers and walls and in building bridges between us.

We are so varied and different, and that should be honoured and praised. Each of us brings individual life experience, personality and opinion. Our cognitive diversity must be treasured, unlocked and harnessed to truly get the best from any team or group of people. The greater the difference of perspective in a team, the more ideas, solutions, ways of thinking and ways of working will be uncovered. Not only that but, by including everyone fully at every level of decision making across an organisation, the sense of belonging both for those within the organisation and those whom the organisation serves will be enhanced. So the questions we all need to consider are thus: who are we building/creating/making things for and who are they being built/created/made by? When we make decisions who are we making them with and who are we making them without? If we want to be the very best we can be as teams, groups and organisations, these are the questions we must answer with honesty and openness.

This book is about people, getting the best out of all people and, in doing so, building exceptional high-performing and successful teams. We cannot know all of our wonderful difference if we don't immerse ourselves in it. And this is why we are raising this point here in our final chapter. We believe that our greatest gift as human beings is our difference. We will never fully know what it is to live another person's life. We feel that, if we actively stay curious and listen to one another's lived experience, it will put us in a much better position to be able to not only function alongside one another but also help make each other better. This is the marker for all great teams and exceptional teammates. When we are our best selves and actively support other people being their best selves, as a team we can thrive. Be the best ally you can be to all people – that is all any of us can ever do.

Team huddle

Your ability to understand, empathise and acknowledge your personal uniqueness and that of your teammates is essential to truly get the best from your team. By embracing your differences and being fully inclusive of every member of your team you will enhance belonging, increase motivation and improve performance output.

Questions to consider

- What are you doing to make sure everyone feels included?
- Is there diversity of thought and life experience in every layer of your organisation?
- How much effort is put into making sure that your talent pipelines are open and accessible to a diverse range of the population?
- How is discrimination addressed?
- Do you and your colleagues all feel that you can speak up about discrimination without fear?
- Are your selection/promotion and hiring processes equitable?
- Does everyone feel like they belong in your team? Who has the strongest and weakest sense of belonging?
- Can people challenge and have contrary opinions without fear of retribution?

Key team tactics

- Go beyond your initial judgement and thoughts about people you work or interact with. We all have biases and we can be conscious of them. We may not be able to unlearn these biases but you can overcome them by creating new habitual thoughts and responses.

- Engage in personality profiling as a foundational tool to open up conversations around our many differences. It can be easier to talk to a report rather than from experience. Use them to break down unhelpful assumptions, stereotypes and tropes. Remember, the profiles are imperfect like us and so should be used in a balanced way and with care.
- Actively engage with people who are different from you. Listen to their stories and be curious about their lived experience.
- Be a good ally to marginalised people and communities; listen, acknowledge privilege, get comfortable with discomfort, amplify voices, learn from your mistakes, call out discrimination, insist on diverse thought at every opportunity.
- Work through our exercises in Chapter 7 to ensure that you fully accept yourself. This acceptance will enhance your ability to be empathetic to other people who are inevitably different from you. We must accept ourselves first before we can truly belong.
- Anonymously measure your team's sense of belonging. Belonging is impacted by how much you feel you can be your whole self without fear or judgement. A team with a strong sense of belonging in all team members will be more motivated, be more engaged, have increased output and perform better.

Final thoughts …

At the beginning of this book we opened with us winning an Olympic gold medal with our teammates in Rio 2016. We hope that, now you've read through this book and worked through some of our Team huddles, you can also see lots of other, perhaps more significant, wins that we experienced on our journey. These wins are there for you, they are there for all of us, and we hope we have inspired you to go after them for yourself and your teammates.

We were at our most successful, both as individuals and as teams, when we were part of empowered cultures that centred around people. In creating an environment that aimed to get the best from every person within it, we gave ourselves the best chance of success as a team and that much needed sense of fulfilment for everybody involved. When we brought our visions, values and behaviours off the page of our books and into real life we created a culture that lived and breathed in all of us. That sense of responsibility, accountability and ownership is key to all teams that really want to win together. Reflect on your team and your culture often, and let this reflection be the guide that leads you to where you want to go.

At the heart of this book is a tremendous amount of care. We cared for what we did, what we were about, and how we wanted to be remembered as hockey players, as people and as teams. We care deeply for our teammates, for what they have taught us, for all that they are and for all that they've shared with us. We also care about you, the reader. We want you to thrive and be the very best version of yourself that you can be. As we continue on our endless journey of self-acceptance and understanding, we hope that by sharing our truth we have helped you feel more at peace with your own. Be kind to yourself and at the same time find that care for others in your life, too. When we give time, energy and effort to supporting other people to thrive we grow so much personally as well. In a team environment all of this care is key to making sure we get all of the knowledge, all of the strengths and all of the value from every team member, and this will ultimately ensure the best chance of success for everyone.

This connection between people is a core ingredient to any successful team. The invaluable bonds of trust and respect that are built through the build-up of many thousands of small moments will help make you strong as a team. The sharing of whole selves, the ability to celebrate all of the small wins together and the collective empathy shown through devastating lows are all things that make you a team – indeed, this is what makes a good team so special. And it is this connectivity and vulnerability that can elevate you from a group of individuals to a highly effective team. That part of us that innately needs to care for people when they open themselves up to us will be the gift that keeps giving as we in turn find the courage to do the same. When the boundaries of the group are well established and safe, it is here we find the deep-rooted sense of belonging that we all desire in life.

An important point to note is that none of what we experienced, or what we talk about in this book, can or should be viewed as a quick fix to any cultural or personal wants or needs. What we created as a team at the Rio Olympic Games may have looked magical – sporting success always does – but the real work was done in the months and years leading up to it. The magic comes from the readiness to be consistent, to give energy and commitment day on day, week on week, month on month and even year on year. There is no secret here or magic bullet, but within our teams, guided by empowering leadership, we have the capacity to create the environments we want to be a part of, if we are willing to put the time and effort into it.

We experienced the ups and the downs of life in a team environment and found deep layers of learning in it all. We were and are still humanly imperfect; we are constantly finding ourselves in a dance with culture, people and teams. There are times when the dance is in step and we're in time, and there are other times when it feels like we've got two left feet and couldn't find the rhythm if we tried. That's life. We are always moving, growing, changing, adapting, failing and winning. That is the dance of a team, and that is the dance of life. Enjoy it all for what it is and what it brings us.

We were excited about writing this book because we're excited about the opportunity it presents for you and the many teams you belong to. We believe that, if teams and the people in them are able to work on and work through everything we have covered in this book, then you can all win. Through this book we wanted to continue on our quest to 'Be the difference, create history and inspire the future', and we hope we have motivated you to do the same.

Acknowledgements

From us both

Our sincerest thanks and deepest respect to all of our GB and England teammates and members of our management teams who are found in between all of the lines of this book. Your brave souls with whom we have shared so much will always be in our hearts. The connections we made, the roller coaster we journeyed along, ensured we belonged then, we belong now and we will belong for ever. Thank you in particular to our teammates who continue to provide lessons for us to learn, space for us to be, and love for us to grow. We are one team.

Special thanks to all of the players and staff who made our efforts for the London and Rio Olympic Games so successful, not just in the results but also in what we created together. Not everyone was there at the start, and some weren't there at the end, but all of you played your part in making us the team we wanted to be and for that we are truly grateful:

Abi Walker, Alex Danson-Bennett (née Danson), Amber Luzar, Amy Gibson, Andrea Furst, Annie Panter, Ashleigh Ball, Beckie Middleton (née Herbert), Becky Duggan, Beth Storry, Ben Rosenblatt, Charlotte Craddock, Chloe Palmer (née Strong), Chloe Rogers, Colin Paterson, Craig Keegan, Craig Parnham, Crista Cullen, Daniel Kings, Danny Kerry, Dave Hamilton, David Faulkner, Deb Smith, Dilly Newton, Ellie Watton, Emily Douglas (née Maguire), Emily Tyrer, Emma

Batchelor, Emma Gardener, Emma Mitchell, Gemma Darring-ton, Gemma Ible, Georgie Twigg, Giselle Ansley, Grace Balsdon, Hannah Macleod, Hilary Rose, Hollie Pearne-Webb (née Webb), Holly Payne, Jo Ellis-Day (née Ellis), John Hurst, Joie Leigh, Karen Brown, Katie Long, Kirsty Shea (née Mackay), Kerry Williams, Laura Staveley (née Bartlett), Laura Unsworth, Lily Owsley, Lucy Wood, Maddie Hinch, Maggie Souyave, Matt Bramhall, Michaela Smith, Mike Rossiter, Morag McLel-lan, Natalie Seymour, Nicola White, Rachel Walker, Rich Beer, Sabbie Heesh, Sally Walton, Sam Quek, Sarah Evans (née Heycroft), Sarah Robertson, Sarah Thomas, Shona McCallin, Sophie Bray, Steph Elliot, Steve Bayer, Susannah Townsend, Susie Catlin (née Gilbert), Tom Cross, Tom Drowley, Vikki Bunce and Zoe Shipperley.

... And thank you to the Rio squad for giving us your blessing to share our team behaviour statements.

To all those courageous people out there who within their own teams continue to go 'all in' even though the going is tough and in the face of multiple failures. The people who have big dreams buried deep who want to push through their fear and shine their light for all to see. And the people who know that as a diverse collective we can achieve magical things when we work together – keep on being amazing.

To Iain Campbell, Robert Tuesley Anderson and the whole team at John Murray Press. If there were prizes awarded for patience, our editor, Iain, would be a deserving winner! Thank you, Iain, for your guidance, time and ever-present energy over the last few years. Your belief that we had something worth sharing was a light for us to cling on to when doubt appeared on the horizon. And to Robert Tuesley Anderson who found time to write a number of his own books while giving his time and care to ours. Thank you, Robert. Your honesty, sincerity and love for the written word were entirely infectious. Hopefully we can meet you in person someday soon.

To Radha Balani – your alternative perspective and vast knowledge were invaluable for us. Thank you for being there for us; we're here for you always.

To Chris Paouros – your ability to find the clarity in our ramblings never ceases to amaze us. You are a phenomenally gifted woman, and we are so grateful to have you in our lives.

To Nick Walters, our book agent – thank you so much for listening to our story, for seeing something in our book that was worth fighting for and for being a brilliant ear over the last few years.

To Lisa Markey and Ben Pilbeam, our agents at Think Beyond – thank you for all of your energy, love and support over the last five years. We have experienced so much together in a relatively short time – you are very much part of our family.

To everyone else at Think Beyond, Molly, Patrick, Nick and the whole team – thank you for your ever-present support and care; it is always very much appreciated.

From Kate

Well, Hels, we did it, we wrote a book! The tortoise pace wins out again! Thank you for being patient with my incessant waffling and never-ending drivel. Your clarity of thought, eye for detail and insatiable knowledge made me write better every day. You make me a better person in every way, every day. I love you so much. Thank you for being all that you are and for loving me the way you do. Let's keep on winning together!

To my loving family – thank you for being there for me no matter what. You have loved and supported me through it all, and I am forever grateful and know that in large part all of this is down to you. All of these years I've been telling you that we're writing a book, and you probably wondered if there was ever going to be one! You inspire me to be me. I love you all with all of my heart always.

From Helen

To Kate – thank you for being an open heart and willing ear to the inner workings of my mind … with no judgement, of course … and a whole heap of patience! I love the realness of you, with no apology – thank you for teaching me to not care so much what others think. I am deeply grateful for what we've shared and continue to share on this crazy ride we call life – here's to winning some more, together.

To my wonderful family – thank you all from the bottom of my heart for your support and encouragement and for loving me just as I am. You instilled in me the courage to be true to myself and give it my all, the confidence to stand up for what I believe in, and the fight to keep going when it got tough. Thank you for being there always, especially when I needed you most – for that I am truly grateful. I love you all.

To Bob, Alan, Dave, Jonesy, Doug, Geoff and all at West Bridgford Hockey Club – thank you for everything. My love for hockey began at your club, as did my basic skills! But you didn't just develop me as a hockey player, you provided my brothers and I with a community, a safe space for us to be, to have fun and to grow as people, whilst being a lifeline for my Mum – there will always be a special place in my heart for you all.

Reading list

Below is a list of the books that have proven useful to us over the years. Some of these books have guided us when we needed them most – some we mentioned within our book and others we haven't specifically quoted but have nevertheless been important reads for us. These authors have made us curious and prompted us to think and have deep discussions about people and teams. To all of you, we say thank you. You have inspired us, consoled us and your books will remain important sources of information and motivation as we continue to move through life.

Angelou, Maya, *I Know Why the Caged Bird Sings* (Random House, 1969)

Brown, Brené, *Daring Greatly: How the Courage to be Vulnerable Transforms the Way We Live, Parent and Lead* (Penguin Putnam, 2012)

Brown, Brené, 'The Power of Vulnerability', TED Talk, available at: www.ted.com/talks/brene_brown_the_power_of_vulnerability?language=en

Coyle, Daniel, *The Culture Code: The Secrets of Highly Successful Groups* (Random House, 2018)

Criado Perez, Caroline, *Invisible Women: Exposing Data Bias in a World Designed for Men* (Random House, 2020)

Dix, Paul, *When the Adults Change, Everything Changes: Seismic Shifts in School Behaviour* (Independent Thinking Press, 2017)

Doyle, Glennon, *Untamed: Stop Pleasing, Start Living* (The Dial Press, 2020)

Eddo-Lodge, Reni, *Why I'm No Longer Talking to White People about Race* (Bloomsbury Publishing, 2017)

Gladwell, Malcolm, *The Tipping Point: How Little Things Can Make a Big Difference* (Little Brown, 2000)

Gordon, Jon, and Smith, Mike, *You Win in the Locker Room First: 7 Cs to Build a Winning Team in Sports Business and Life* (Wiley, 2015)

Halberstam, David, *The Education of a Coach* (Hyperion Acquired Assets, 2006)

Jackson, Phil, *Eleven Rings: The Legendry MBA Coach Shares the Secrets Behind His Leadership and Success* (Virgin Books, 2015)

Kerr, James, *Legacy: What the All Blacks Can Teach Us about the Business of Life* (Constable, 2013)

Lencioni, Patrick, *The Five Dysfunctions of a Team: A Leadership Fable* (John Wiley & Sons, 2002)

Syed, Matthew, *Black Box Thinking: Marginal Gains and the Secrets of High Performance* (John Murray, 2016)

Tolle, Eckhart, *A New Earth: Create a Better Life* (Penguin, 2009)

Trescothick, Marcus, *Coming Back to Me* (HarperSport, 2009)

Walsh, Bill, *The Score Takes Care of Itself: My Philosophy of Leadership* (Portfolio, 2010)

Index